THE SPIRIT OF REVOLT

The Spirit of Revolt

Richard K. Fenn

ROWMAN & LITTLEFIELD
PUBLISHERS

ROWMAN & LITTLEFIELD

Published in the United States of America in 1986
by Rowman & Littlefield, Publishers
(a division of Littlefield, Adams & Company)
81 Adams Drive, Totowa, New Jersey 07512

Library of Congress Cataloging-in-Publication Data

Fenn, Richard K.
  The spirit of revolt.

  Bibliography: p. 173
  Includes index.
  1. Secularism. 2. Authority. 3. Social psychology.
I. Title.
BL2747.8.F464   1986   303   86-15430
ISBN 0-8476-7522-X

89 88 87 86
10 9 8 7 6 5 4 3 2 1

Printed in the United States of America

Contents

Acknowledgments

My FIRST AND GREATEST DEBT is to my family; I cannot describe it here but happily acknowledge it. My colleague at the University of Maine, Burt Hatlen, was very helpful in giving some direction to my reading in anarchist thought and generous in lending books from his library. Colleagues in England, Bryan Wilson and David Martin, have read parts of this book in earlier versions, and by their comments and criticism have made me question my own assumptions and commitments. My daughter Caroline has helped with suggestions and by sharing her own perspective on anarchism.

Over several years I have been helped in a variety of ways by the members of two mutual-aid societies, the Association for the Sociology of Religion, and the Society for the Scientific Study of Religion. They have provided a context and a climate in which the notion of a secular society has come alive even though the concept remains problematical. I owe too many of their members various debts to begin listing individuals by name.

Sue McLaughlin, at the University of Maine, has provided typing and editorial assistance with far more patience and tact than I could have asked for.

For permission to reprint portions of the Introduction, I wish to thank the editor of Sociological Analysis; they appeared in Volume 6, No. 4 (Winter 1986).

For permission to reprint portions of Chapter 6, I wish to thank the editor of the Princeton Seminary Bulletin; they appeared in Volume VII, No. 1.

For permission to reprint portions of Robert and Ann Coles's *Women in Crisis: Lives of Struggle and Hope,* I wish to thank Dell Publishers.

Richard K. Fenn

vii

Introduction

THE NOTION OF A SECULAR SOCIETY still attracts sociologists. Indeed, as Wilson (1985) argues, the task of sociology from the outset has been to give an adequate account of secularization as a social process that first became highly visible primarily in Western societies and now impinges on virtually every nation. Although the pace of secularization varies from one time and place to another, the process continues. Wilson (ibid.) further notes that the process is compatible with a considerable amount of resistance. Movements to revitalize cultures and to restore ancestral faiths may for a time encompass whole societies. Individual religiosity also may survive, and whole groups may define themselves and claim recognition on religious grounds. The process, indeed, may be reversible; as Wilson notes, it is too soon to say. That it is the task of sociology (and not merely of the sociology of religion) to give an account of the process of secularization, Wilson has no doubt, and I firmly agree. Even though his article, to which I have been referring, appears in a volume whose editor announces that the notion of secularization has been discredited, rumors of the death of this idea are usually premature.

The idea of secularization is abstract and controversial. Because it is an abstract notion, there are many, more concrete ideas that can be derived from it. All the evidence that can be compiled on religious revivals in modern societies can be interpreted as signs of negative reactions to the process of secularization: reactions that are likely to fade when the groups protesting get a larger share of social credit or political influence. So much for notions of a "resurgence" of religion. Furthermore, the idea of secularization is controversial precisely because groups and individuals do find their ideas and values reflected or subverted in discussions of the theory itself. Intellectuals who are committed to certain "ultimate values" are no less likely than social classes committed to ascetic lifestyles to deplore a theory that relegates such commitments to rearguard holding actions against a process that makes problem

1

solving and the management of social conflict a largely pragmatic enterprise devoid of ultimate significance and value. So controversial and abstract a notion as secularization is likely to generate interest and debate without leading to a clear intellectual victory for any of the parties involved.

In this book, I hope to clarify at least one of the options in the debate: to make clear the grounds for one position that has been somewhat neglected among sociologists. Here I will develop a notion of secularization that differs in important respects from the model that has been the object of so much confusion and controversy. For lack of a better word, I will call that model, of which Wilson is one of the foremost proponents, the priestly model, while the one I wish to develop here might be called—for the sake of comparison—the prophetic paradigm. This is a distinction that is sometimes used in sociology to distinguish two types of models or paradigms: two different ways of envisioning how the disparate facts of a community or society hang together. It would be desirable, in another book, to develop a systematic comparison of the two points of view and to apply them both to the solution of a single problem. Here I have chosen simply to develop only the prophetic viewpoint on secularization rather than to engage in debates over the relative merits of the theories that can be derived from the two paradigms.

The more familiar, "priestly" view of secularization regards societies as the voice of reason and locates in individuals the emotions and values, the impulses and the prejudices that impede "the rationalization of external social order" (Wilson, 1985). In this view, the process of secularization may be in the hands of a priestly class. To begin with, it was the shaman in primitive communities who supplied the voice of reason. Through ritual and prayer, as well as through considerable force of persuasion, the shaman was able to quiet panic and introduce order into a social life that was frequently disrupted by outbursts of fear or by demands for satisfaction and revenge. To a modern eye, rituals of exorcism might seem irrational; to the primitive, they were indeed the voice of reason. To drive out spirits and to counter witchcraft were necessary steps if a community were to ward off evil and to avoid disaster that would overwhelm individual defenses and create panic.

Whether the sacred fosters or impedes the process of secularization therefore depends on particular factors of time and place. In medieval societies, as Wilson notes, priestly classes continued to be the voice of reason. Granted that they spoke on behalf of a sacred universe, it was a universe that required logic and tended to exclude the unpredictable and the disruptive. Wilson's point is precisely that secularization does introduce order into "the fears, hopes, fantasies, the search for meaning and wish-fulfillment, and the encapsulation of these tendencies in folk-lore and local custom" (ibid.). That is why the priestly classes, especially in Christianity, have been hostile to local magic and tradition. The opposition of the churches to the traditions of indigenous peoples in Europe or elsewhere has been no less severe than the churches' former opposition to science and technology. The question has always been who is to represent the dominant voice of reason.

The "priestly" model of the process of secularization therefore casts different actors in the role of reason, but the plot remains what Wilson calls "the rationalization of external social order." In the most advanced societies, that voice speaks most persuasively through administrators and law-makers, scientists, and other experts who seek to make institutions relatively immune from surprise, popular fashion, and the demand for revenge. No wonder that the churches have increasingly found themselves supporting the local and popular traditions that they once attacked when the churches spoke for the prevailing form of social order. It is only a relatively recent historical development, however, that pits science or formal law against religion. The same process has often been carried out through classes whose interests in order were expressed through a sacred universe that supplied the principles on which reason would work in law, education, science, and the family. It is only a question of which classes enjoy the privilege of speaking for "the rationalization of external social order," as Wilson put it. Sociologists who are disenchanted with the priestly model of secularization are nonetheless operating entirely within its premises when they identify religion with the forces in modern society that are likely to attack the rule of scientific experts or demand that the law accomodate their specific traditions in the family and the school.

The literature on theories of secularization is as full of controversy as the courts, and it would be interesting to describe that controversy in more detail. That task, however, has already been undertaken a number of times in the last ten years without ending the confusion in current debates over how secular the modern world really is (cf. Glasner 1977; Johnson 1979; Dobbelaere, 1981). Here I will not attempt to sort out various "theories" of secularization, since this work does not really attempt such a theory in itself. A theory, after all, attempts to give such an adequate account of certain relationships that one can venture to say something like this: "As the political or economic system becomes more secular, religion not only tends to lose influence in the making of decisions in those spheres but becomes more politicized and more intensely popular." Such a theory could relate concepts like secularization and religion in terms specific enough to allow for systematic historical or comparative investigations of the type recently and effectively engaged in by David Martin (1978). In this book, however, I am seeking to describe what a secular society would be if a set of conditions is actually met, rather than to debate the relative merits of the paradigms or to develop another theory.

Most of the theories of secularization over which there is still so much controversy stem from the "priestly" paradigm. For instance, that paradigm focuses on what Wilson (1985) calls "the rationalization of external social order." Whatever excludes the intense emotions or values that threaten to interrupt or disrupt social order is itself secularizing. The forces of order may at one time include the sacred, with a more or less complete set of professionals, rites, belief-systems, and institutions. On the other hand, religious professionals and their panoply of support may threaten to overwhelm the institutions that guarantee a modicum of order. In either event, religion may not only inhibit or support secularization; it may disguise or express social tendencies toward secularization. The task of describing a society in these terms is therefore just as complicated as the task of explaining why things turn out the way they do. There is enough disagreement among sociologists over whether American democratic values are really secular or covertly religious to fuel debates for another generation; at the same time, sociologists may continue to speculate over whether modern American religious movements are really "religious" or covertly secular in their values and goals.

The tasks of explanation, definition, and illustration in this field are complex, and there are frequent attempts to reduce such conceptual complexity by reaching a rough-and-ready consensus on terms. Benton Johnson (1979), for instance, tries to capture "whatever agreement there may be in our field" by *defining secularization* "as a process of change that involves a decline of the supernatural element in systems of meaning." Earlier, however, Roland Robertson (1972) suggested that sociologists *define religion* in terms of supernatural belief-systems in order to investigate whether—and under what conditions—secularization causes a decline in religion. In other words, Robertson left open the theoretical question that Johnson seeks to close by definition. Intellectual responsibility, I would suggest, requires that sociologists keep open the theoretical question of how religion fosters or responds to secularization. That question, however, lies considerably beyond what I am attempting here, which is merely to lay out an alternative paradigm for grasping the elements of secularization in a way that the priestly paradigm, with its emphasis on order, tends to preempt.

A shift from one paradigm to another is often subtle and can easily be missed. Wilson could have written the following description of the process of secularization, but he did not.

> In the first industrial revolution the organic bonds were broken between the vertical links on a personal hierarchy, social and religious; now in the second industrial revolution the horizontal bonds also are broken. The dense, intimate linkages of horizontal community, working class or otherwise, are corroded. Local networks are dispersed and people are up-ended in tower blocks. The small shop gives way to the supermarket; the local school gives way to the comprehensive factory; the moderate-sized office is swallowed up on large-scale bureaucracy; the family firm disappears in the international consortium. The remaining bonds are those of interest rather than solidarity and the psychic economy of the individual turns more around the calculus of gratification. Neither political dogma nor religious community take the individual away from his private future (Pawley, 1973). Neither voluntary association nor religious association excite his private preference. Three great pillars of belonging are corroded: national sentiment, religious community, political solidarity, leaving behind the wrack of group advantage and personal gratification. The structure of communication links the individual antennae with everywhere in general and nobody in particular. It ensures sensory mobility and personal passivity. Religion ceases to be either the necessary bond of all community or part of the web of voluntary association (David Martin 1981:12).

Like Wilson, Martin knows that in the process of secularization "religion becomes one specific sector not the essence of the whole" and "the casing of thought ceases to be theological" (ibid.:10). The division of labor, he notes, replaces the divine office with the government office, and sacred ministry is replaced by the "ministry of labour" (1981: 10–11). Like Wilson, he notes that religion is peripheral in a society whose order is based on principles of rationality that exclude hope, tears, and human affection.

With Martin, however, this principle of order is profoundly destructive; note his frequent use of terms like "gives way," "swal-
lowed up," and "disappears." The principle of order in a modern
society is more like a vacuum than a ruler; worlds have been
absorbed, destroyed, and turned into waste matter.

The shift in paradigm comes out more strongly, perhaps, in this
passage from Martin.

> Mobile social space dissolves the cycle of home and market, home
> and plot. Inside that space there is a constant revolution of dis-
> placed persons encountering the relativity of all their worlds. Some-
> how they have to restabilize their expanding relativised worlds and
> so they band themselves together in social movements. Mobility
> creates movements. These movements reorganize time by first
> destroying the timeless cycles and then opening up a secular
> trajectory: the historical career (1981:11).

Here Martin's use of the term secular connotes a world that is
passing away, temporal, finite, and limited finally only by death:
the root senses of the term as referring to an era or epoch, a
bounded zone of historical time that is already doomed to death
by the advent of a reality that does not pass away.

In this second paradigm, there is no single principle of order
typified by a rationalized social system; on the contrary, the social
system itself is an arena in which various orders compete and
temporarily prevail. Each of these orders, moreover, may well
attempt to resemble—or take on the functions previously offered—by religion itself. As Martin puts it, "the political party
now doubles for religion and can even, like religion, seek to
double for the state" (1981:11). There is a shift here, of course, to a
more inclusive notion of religion, but the terminological differences also reflect a shift in paradigm from one that sees order as
central to one that sees only a constant movement of parties and
agencies, each of which competes for a temporary advantage over
the others and offers the individual only a very partial satisfaction
of desires for a certain, if limited, sense of direction. Obligations in
such a society are exceedingly limited, temporary, and specific,
since so little of social life endures. If religion is peripheral to such
a social system, it is because the system, if it can be called that,
makes every institution and individual somehow peripheral to all
the others. The question is not whether the center of such a
system can hold against the intrusions and interruptions of various political, emotional, or religious enthusiasms. There is no
center: there is only a state that manages a semblance of control
over competing classes, corporations, and other interests.

Until the differences between these two paradigms become clear, it will not be of much use to call for more precise definitions or more systematically garnered facts. We might agree that it is reasonable to speak of political parties as carrying out religious functions, but this agreement in terms would not produce a consensus in theory so long as some sociologists are using the priestly paradigm and others the prophetic. A political party that carries out the functions of religion in providing faith and hope, if not charity, may be acting in support of—or against—a system that is dominated by a single principle of order; under these conditions, secularization would mean approximately what Wilson has in mind, and the role of religion might both support or subvert that principle. On the other hand, if political parties are providing religious functions in a society that has no single principle of order, the role of religion (whether one speaks of beliefs, political parties, or church organizations) is far harder to assess. Relationships between "church and state" hardly typify the relation of religion to society, and society itself is difficult to typify except in negative terms as the absence of a cultural sense or consensus or as the presence of forces that, as Martin might have put it, destroy one another on contact. A society is evanescent in which obligations tend to be highly specific, limited, and likely to disappear over time. Using the same paradigm to examine changes in a single society or to make comparisons between different societies might therefore introduce serious distortions when only a shift in paradigms can adequately document the shift from a system in which external social order is rationalized to one that lacks such an external principle.

It is dangerous to assess the role of religion in a society that may once have embodied a dominant principle of order and has subsequently lost it. The sociologist might then be tempted to overestimate the religious significance of national symbols or the religious function of national organizations, many of them political, in a modern society, because the same symbols and functions had sustained (or subverted) the principle by which that society was ordered at an earlier time. Whether the sociologist thinks of those symbols as sustaining the society in its modern state or as having been crudely ignored or "broken," the bias is toward an overestimation of their importance to the ordering of the nation's life. No amount of fact-gathering and no strain toward rigorous definition will solve the problem caused by inappropriate use of paradigms. The question is always "the goodness of fit," so to speak, of the one paradigm or the other.

The simplest questions about the interpretation of religious behavior depend on which paradigm one is using. A society may be "secular" because its primary ordering principle is rational, or a society may be "secular" because it has no primary ordering principle. In the former case, figures on church attendance may be indications of the degree to which people are happy or unhappy with the larger society; much depends on the kinds of people and the kinds of churches they attend. In any case, however, their attendance would probably reflect the rationality on the basis of which the larger society is organized. If their local churches used symbols that also could be found in the political or cultural center, their religion could signify that they assent to the dominant order, which would leave little room for the disruption of social life by impulse and by self-assertion. Under these circumstances religion serves civic purposes, and its critics tend to argue that religion has survived at the cost of an inner secularization. The critical point is usually moot, since it depends on judgments that are partially theological and partially aesthetic. The sociological point, how-ever, is that the society in question is ordered to the extent that it makes the serendipitous socially marginal.

On the other hand, in such a society religious groups might signify a certain hostility to the habits and privileges of local or national elites, and the people might exhibit a piety, enthusiasm, or asceticism in their way of life that enabled them to score moral victories over other more fortunate but also more corruptible citizens. Even under these circumstances, however, it is possible to speak of religion as surviving, even thriving as an alternative to a society that is secular precisely because it has contained or thwarted piety and enthusiasm. Critics could argue that certain religious groups were peripheral or marginal to such a society, or that their religion alone had the courage of the larger society's convictions. In that regard, church attendance by a few might be an outward and visible sign of the latent convictions of the many or of a residue of belief which, once mobilized, might carry an entire nation through a time of crisis. In any event, whether religion symbolizes the center or marks the periphery of social life, there is indeed a cultural center and an emotional or spiritual periphery.

In fact, most sociological descriptions of religion assume that such a fundamental ordering principle does run through the institutions and agencies of the larger society; otherwise there would be no sense in using the term "society." The first paradigm, in other words, contains most of what passes for theoretical agreement or controversy on the role of religion in modern societies. The controversies persist, however, and I suspect they will not be resolved until sociologists consider using the prophetic rather than the priestly paradigm for organizing their observations on religion in modern societies.

It is quite understandable that sociologists who adopt the priestly paradigm fear individualism and the atrophy of a keen sense of the individual's obligations not only to immediate friends and family but to the larger society. Their basic theme sounds a note of warning that modern societies will not long survive if they produce individuals who cannot describe their origin and situation in terms that remind them of their debt to a larger society. A society that cannot make up its mind about the obligations of its members will be confusing at best, and at worst, chaotic or tyrannical.

On the other hand, sociologists have always been alert to the exploitative aspect of any social obligation. Every moral consensus serves some classes or interests better than others; every tie that binds also creates a safe distance between the more and the less privileged or prestigious members of a society. Worse yet, social obligation taken too seriously inhibits the development of individuals who can take full responsibility even for actions that are obligatory; the individual acting in good faith according to a conscience too heavily imbued with received but limited notions of liability ends up acting in "bad faith" (cf. Berger 1963).

Even when one takes social obligations with a critical grain of salt, of course, one can still have a mind or imagination too constrained to think of actions and alternatives that are capable of transforming a society. For instance, it is part of the repertoire of criticism to fault social obligations that bind individuals into subordinate or unfair relationships; far less attention is devoted to studying the possibility of a society without even such a dominant institution as the state. The question, for both the critical and the conservative traditions in sociology, simply concerns which social relationships should be the source or object or a sense of obligation. In other words, sociology lacks a paradigmatic view of a system that lacks any form of social obligation beyond the most immediate, temporary, and specific.

Given an alternative paradigm, it will be possible to widen the debate on secularization. There is widespread agreement that the process of secularization weakens all forms of traditional or customary obligations, e.g., those that have provided more than merely legal, pragmatic, or utilitarian justifications for the authority of the state or of particular professions and institutions. On the basis of the prophetic paradigm, one might go on to argue that these same institutions, e.g., medicine, law, education, and even the state can function quite adequately with more limited and specific sets of obligations that define the role of doctor and patient, citizen and official. The priestly paradigm suggests, however, that no such institution can long survive without borrowing authority from beyond its own precincts or creating obligations not limited to specific transactions. Many sociologists, therefore, still tend to assume that legitimacy cannot be based on effectiveness alone: an assumption that leads to a persistent search for sources of legitimacy in hypothetical and elusive forms of "the sacred." If debates among sociologists of religion have been a bit fruitless, it is perhaps because such debates operate within too limited a set of questions and assumptions; until these limits are broken, the debates will remain unnecessarily circular and inconsequential.

What I call the "prophetic" paradigm questions whether any particular social obligation is rational or necessary. It suggests that the process of secularization proceeds much more rapidly at times when certain obligations have been successfully challenged or have lost their coercive authority over the mind of the individual. When a temple is destroyed or an orthodoxy challenged, a wide range of social obligations becomes questionable or even impossible to fulfill. The transition from a belief in magic and from the hope for a millenium to a secular society (Wilson 1973) therefore moves toward obligations that are increasingly immediate, specific, and temporary.

The prophetic paradigm would accept Durkheim's familiar argument that individuals owe their very lives to society, but it would not follow that this debt should be repaid in a lively sense of the individual's social obligations. I have noted that the priestly paradigm fits a social system that regards moral obtuseness or self-centered activity as dangerous expressions of individualism or narcissism. Sociologists who operate within that paradigm may also interpret an individual's preference for the most limited of engagements with institutions as unhealthy for the individual and for the larger society. A prophetic paradigm would suggest, however, that such a preference for the most limited of engagements makes sense when institutions are greedy, their expertise based on shifting assumptions and information, and when authorities themselves have chronic problems in claiming credibility and trustworthiness.

If, as some would argue, the legal framework makes it possible for such authorities and institutions to provide goods and services to a population; and if, furthermore, there is a tendency on the part of some to revere such a framework in itself, there will be a tendency over time for the system itself and its most pervasive symbols to become transcendent, the object of some veneration, and the source of moral obligation to the society as a whole. Sociologists operating from the prophetic paradigm may well regard such a development as a sign of social pathology.

There is some precedent in the psychoanalytic literature for such diagnosis. A sense of obligation to the dead becomes, in the work of Robert Lifton, a sign of guilt; that is the familiar interpretation of his work with the survivors of Hiroshima and the Vietnam War. By a simple extension of the same logic to the ordinary citizen, one can question every sense of traditional or customary obligation. If it is pathological for a survivor to feel obligated to those who have perished in some disaster, it is no less pathological for the average citizen to feel that life itself imposes a debt to preceding generations whose sufferings have fostered the continuity of social life. One can simply feel obligated to preceding generations for the fact that one is indeed alive. It is as if one's own life were purchased at the expense of theirs. One can also feel an obligation to share their fate, which is mortality itself. If one's life is a gift, then one has a debt to pay to society; one's life is, so to speak, a loan that can be recalled. The religious equivalent of such logic is very familiar indeed. Applied to the social system and the legacy of preceding generations, the same logic leaves the individual with a residual sense of guilt and a chronic sense of obligation that may require the forfeiture of the individual's own life. The state has traded on such guilt for centuries, and in calling for more individuals to sacrifice their lives has provided ample opportunity for their survivors to feel that they too have an added debt to be discharged, if need be, with their own lives. Such a circle is vicious; from the prophetic viewpoint, it is pathological.

The prophetic paradigm does not minimize the dangers of narcissism and individualism. Certainly the sociology of religion appreciates that the institution of religion, broadly defined, seeks to control and to fulfill the individual's desire to be at the center and source of life. To be reminded that God alone creates "out of nothing" may indeed help to control the magical and grandiose thinking that accompanies childhood narcissism. Western religion also reminds one that there is a fundamental flaw, an original sin in existence itself. On the one hand, no one can live without the support and correction of others; on the other hand, a sense of the self as whole and complete cannot fully be obtained through the responses of others. God alone provides those reflections on the self that can restore a full image of what it means to be human. Certain types of religion seek to inhibit grandiose narcissism, then, and offer the individual a self-image that is essentially hidden in the mind of God.

Anarchist, psychoanalytic, and theological approaches to narcissism are sources for the prophetic paradigm. They locate the danger posed by narcissism to both society and the individual in the individual's attempt to be more than what one is at the moment. It is not narcissism per se that destroys the social fabric, but narcissism inflated by grandiose thinking, by the infinite expansion of the self, and by the attempt to coerce the response of others. The task is always to recognize others as being "Other," and theology justifies the limiting experience of the Other as the legacy of a "Fall." Indeed, with little variation over the last twenty centuries, Christianity has outlawed what Zweig (1968, 1980) aptly calls "the heresy of self-love." It is a heresy, Zweig notes, that has taken new form with the discovery of the vast and impersonal spaces of nature in which humans neither figure centrally or reign; no wonder that poetic and philosophic imaginations have been prompted to reorder the universe from skeptical reason and from the most carefully cultivated inner sensibilities (1968, 1980:125–41). In such a secular cosmos, there appears to be no sacred space or sanctuary other than that created in the vastness of the individual's own mind. That is, indeed, heresy for orthodox Christianity, and madness when divorced from an awareness of the outside world as organized according to laws that have no one particularly in mind. In such a world, as an alternative to either despair or grandiosity, a limited notion of social obligations would appear to be humane as well as simply realistic: humane, because it imposes no heroic responsibility and realistic because it recognizes no extraordinary destiny for the individual.

Exaggerated notions of social obligation have their origins in a pathology of the mind; psychoanalysis and religion are relatively clear on this point. True enough of individuals, it is true at least by analogy of nations. A case in point is provided by the religious aspects of a nation's identity. Much has already been written, for instance, on the subject of the United States' assurance of its own special place among the nations: one marked by an exceptional destiny that also carries with it exceptional obligations. Oddly enough, this high calling carries with it not only the obligation to be the vehicle of a providential mission in history but also a license to pursue life, liberty, and happiness. Some sociologists have chosen to explain this apparent contradiction by referring to Protestantism and to the Enlightenment as polar aspects of Americans' cultural inheritance; however, historians like John Wilson (1979) rightly argue that such reasoning fails to see the hedonistic and religious aspects of American culture as part of the same constellation of symbols. This constellation or complex joins a highly exceptional sense of America's social obligations (and of Americans' obligations, therefore to their nation) with a very grand sense of the individual's rights (to pursue life, liberty, and happiness). Such a complex at the level of the nation is no less pathological, I would suggest, than at the level of the individual.

To understand the point, however, it may help to consider Freud's discussion of a particular case of a young man who thought of himself as exceptional. The young man in question displayed the same constellation or complex of characteristics that I have just mentioned in connection with the religious aspects of America's national destiny; he felt himself singled out for a special destiny and watched over by a special providence (Freud 1963:159–60). Like other patients who considered themselves exceptional, he resisted the notion that he must suffer even "a provisional renunciation of any source of pleasure . . ." (Freud 1963:158). The special providence that watched over this young man "would protect him from any painful sacrifices of the sort" (ibid.:159). Eventually, Freud unearthed what lay behind this notion of a special providence and of a right to exact satisfaction from the world—an early, accidental infection that he had acquired from the one upon whom he most depended for nourishment, his wet nurse (ibid.:160). As Bellah (1967) has pointed out, an essential part of the religious symbols of American identity refer to times of suffering and testing as part of a providential plan for this exceptional nation; no wonder that the people also have enshrined their right to some extraordinary satisfactions hitherto beyond the reach of the majority of mortals. The priestly paradigm locates a principle of order in the sense of social obligations incumbent on the nation or on its citizens; the prophetic paradigm suggests that this principle conceals and yet expresses a heightened notion of what a people feel is owed to them. The sociologist operating from within the prophetic paradigm is more likely to analyze rather than to propound the meaning of such a complex. In the end, a prophetic view of the individual's or of the nation's social obligations may emerge and recommend itself, which is both reasonable and human rather than heroic and, ultimately, disappointing.

To develop the prophetic paradigm, I draw frequently for inspiration not only on the psychoanalytical and theological literature but also on the legacy of anarchist thought. To the anarchists, primitive societies seemed blessed, but also hopeless in the extreme: blessed because primitives understood cooperation, sacrifice, courage, mutual aid, and the spontaneous creation of their own life through ritual and technical experimentation; hopeless because primitives were prone to fear, superstition, to the sanctification of routine, and to the dread of change (cf. Kropotkin 1927, 1970:203–05). Sociologists using the priestly paradigm might very well agree with Max Weber that the tendency to submit to routine and to sacrifice one's own independence is a *given* in human nature; modern soceities, through a bureaucratized state, only enhance that primitive proclivity for helplessness. As for the primitives' capacity to create and recreate their own social conditions, Weber thought that such capacity would increasingly depend on charismatic leadership or, at best, on the various forms of prophecy that could unsettle and briefly disturb the routines of an administered society; the doors of the iron cage had been shut forever, even though some might try to rattle those doors from time to time. Kropotkin, however, attributes such pessimism to an education that "seeks to kill in us the spirit of revolt and to develop that of submission to authority"; indeed, "our society seems no longer able to understand that it is possible to exist otherwise than under the reign of law, elaborated by a representative government, and administered by a handful of rulers" (1927, 1970:197). Even if our society has lost the capacity for such a sociological imagination, should sociologists not keep such an imagination alive?

In developing a notion of a secular society from the prophetic viewpoint, I therefore accept Kropotkin's suggestion that even the state itself is dispensable and is sustained only by the various institutions that contribute to a "cult of authority." More importantly, the anarchist program challenges sociology to consider the possibility of a society based on minimal obligations: in short, the possibility of a wholly secularized social system based only on the most immediate, temporary, and specific forms of authority.

The prophetic paradigm raises the question whether any cult of authority need or can survive; anarchists assume that all such cults must be terminated in any event if peoples are truly to be free. There will always be authority, but in a free society such authority is not mystified, concentrated, institutionalized, or offered the sacrifices of the purse, the intellect, or of the will. A truly secular society would be one in which authority is only—and entirely—functional in its significance; expertise would not be the object of moral obligation or the source of moral authority. This point is lost, however, when sociologists assume that all social order is also a moral order. Of course, many roles are also agencies because they serve to control behavior in some way that is important to the continuity and well-being of a social system. Every control function depends on some definition of rights and responsibilities; every such definition, furthermore, is normative and invokes a sense of what is understood to be right or wrong. The priestly paradigm therefore tends to assume that all agents and agencies of a society rest on cultural grounds that are ethical or religious rather than temporary and pragmatic. The prophetic paradigm is open to the notion of a society in which all authority is the result of continuous negotiation, i.e., is wholly deinstitution-alized.

The process of secularization involves the decline of authority in virtually every area of modern American society, a point made by many sociologists who operate from a priestly rather than prophetic viewpoint. Take, for instance, the work of Lasch (1979) on the "culture of narcissism." Hardly an anarchist in his sympathies, Lasch describes the eclipse of authority that rests on moral or religious grounds, on the grounds of custom and tradition, or even on the grounds of a clear and substantive expertise. The public ignores its customs and forgets its traditions; the Constitution and the liberal ethos itself become foreign to a public raised on inoperative statements and swamped with information. Unable to "suspend disbelief" when faced with authorities in the home or at school, no one suspends disbelief when listening to the last press release from the White House. Politics becomes entertainment, but entertainment loses its capacity to enthrall and enchant.

Under these conditions, I would argue, the prophetic paradigm is likely to have more "goodness of fit" than the priestly. A society so secularized that no authority can claim allegiance or capture the imagination leaves every individual a "free agent." Under these conditions, no forms of respect or allegiance that suppress individual initiative or require sacrifice will long endure. These losses of meaning and of culturally based personal identity are indicative of advanced levels of secularization. To mourn their passing, as Lasch does, makes sense from within the priestly paradigm, perhaps, but the prophetic alternative offers a positive assessment of the structure of a modern society based on such minimal and transitory forms of social obligation.

In appraising Lasch's argument, therefore, it would be useful to adopt Kropotkin's notion of a society in which the cult of authority has been replaced by mutual aid and by the freedom of the individual to grow, to mature, to live, and to die on his or her own terms:

Acknowledging, as a fact, the equal rights of its members to the treasures accumulated in the past, it no longer recognizes a division between exploited and exploiters, governed and governors, dominated and dominators, and it seeks to establish a certain harmonious compatibility in its midst—not by subjecting all its members to an authority that is fictitiously supposed to represent society, not by trying to establish uniformity, but by urging all men to develop free initiative, free action, free association.

It seeks the most complete development of individuality combined with the highest development of voluntary association in all its aspects, in all possible degrees, for all imaginable aims; ever changing, ever modified associations which carry in themselves the elements of their durability and constantly assume new forms which answer best to the multiple aspirations of all.

A society to which pre-established forms, crystallized by law, are repugnant; which looks for harmony in an ever-changing and fugitive equilibrium between a multitude of varied forces and influences of every kind, following their own course . . . (Kropotkin 1927, 1970:123–24).

Studies of secularization need not result in Lasch's despairing analyses of the decline of authority, but can point to possibilities for freedom and for voluntary associations that are only beginning to appear. Just as anarchists unfavorably compared modern societies with the medieval city, Weber also found in that occidental city a model for the integration of an increasingly complex society through free exchange and through responsibilities for social solidarity, self-determination, free association, a minimum of regulation, a maximum of creativity, and a generalized set of political commitments that ensure that individual decisions will be compatible with, if not conducive to, the relatively smooth functioning of the society as a whole. The prophetic question is where the possibilities for such freedom and solidarity can be located in the modern nation-state.

Dobbelaere's (1985) excellent and exhaustive analysis of various sociologists' views of secularization documents not only the complexity of the subject but the negative "priestly" view of the role of the individual in secular societies. Individuals are no longer "cultural dupes" who unwittingly serve the larger society under the delusion that they are pursuing their own liberty and happiness. Societal purposes have been abstracted, placed to one side, or exhausted to the point that modern societies are now living on "borrowed capital": an insight Dobbelaere derives quite appropriately from Bryan Wilson. Instead of being duped by their culture, individuals are now duped, he argues, by the complex structure of the societies in which they live.

Dobbelaere's discussion suggests how individuals are increasingly adopting the most immediate, specific, and temporary of obligations in the more secularized societies without expanding their degrees of freedom. (1) Individuals now *achieve* their place(s) in modern societies rather than having most of their places assigned to them by less immediately relevant, ascribed characteristics. (2) Principles of equal rights entitle individuals to select roles in one sector of a society regardless of their roles elsewhere. (3) The range of choice is somewhat narrowed, however, by the requirements pertinent to specific roles; a certain level of experience or competence may be required for access to a particular role. (4) The range of choice is further narrowed, once one occupies a role, by the fact that others are players in the same or in related games; (for instance, individuals who farm must be oriented to an array of actors who are preoccupied with banking, insurance, interest rates, or with gambling on the future prices of specific commodities). (5) The range of freedom is further constrained by the fact that individuals must frequently ignore the interests or values they hold as occupants of other roles; (public officials are expected, if not always required, to forget who has loaned them money, while candidates for high office are expected to remember such things). (6) Where institutions do not provide the necessary constraints to blind individuals to their interests as occupants of roles elsewhere in the society, individuals are expected to constrain themselves; this is what is meant by an ethic of individual responsibility. The rationalization of the social system, on this priestly view, does make the truly personal aspects of the individual irrelevant and inappropriate to any roles in which the individual acts as an agent of the system.

The net result, as Dobbelaere points out, is to make decisions less a private matter than highly "individuated": i.e., immediate, specific, and temporary but lacking in substantive freedom and constrained by an increasingly rationalized social order. (7) As societies become increasingly complex, each role impinges on other roles, each actor affects a wide range of other individuals who are not among his or her acquaintances, and the so called private sphere diminishes. (8) As the private sphere diminishes, societies develop an increasingly high stake in limiting individual discretion while requiring individuals to become increasingly discrete. (9) In looking for cultural resources to enable individuals to become increasingly "responsible," societies may turn to various professions as agencies of social control; for instance, American society has assigned an increasingly important role to the therapeutic professions in managing problems stemming from individual decision-making. Religious professionals have also been engaged in a wide range of chaplaincies, but, as Dobbelaere (1985:10) points out, they work within institutions that increasingly have difficulty in defining themselves as religious. A further source of social control is the ethic of professionalization, through which virtually everyone claims the responsibilities and, therefore, the rights once monopolized by a relatively few highly regarded professions. Under these conditions, individuals cannot be sure of the extent of their freedom and responsibility, but they must act "as if" they are both free and responsible. In the priestly view, secularization not only makes individuality superfluous in all but the most superficial aspect; it requires that individuals accept these limitations with good graces.

Understood from within the priestly paradigm, the religion of the churches or the protesting religion of various social movements will only illustrate various strategies for encompassing their situations of relatively limited and ambiguous freedom in a highly complex bureaucratized society. The prophetic paradigm, however, offers an analytical alternative on the basis of which to assess the degrees of freedom and social obligation seized and lost in response to these social (and existential) conditions. Movements toward freedom and solidarity may have sold their birthright of social power for a greater degree of religious freedom. By displacing conflict from the system itself into subsystems more amenable to religious control, even movements of dissent may have accepted too uncritically the priestly view of secular societies as a rationalized external order impervious to individual hopes and an ultimate nature.

The prophetic paradigm raises the question of what a society might become if its character is no longer shaped by its myths and rituals or by a rationalized principle of order. Secularization itself also makes it reasonable to ponder which forms of economic or political domination will soon lose their authority and which new generation will work for more egalitarian forms of social organization. Secular societies already have fostered a science of individual consciousness that looks on character as a defense and promotes more flexible and satisfying forms of selfhood and individuality; psychoanalysis promises not only a therapeutic adjustment to unalterable social conditions but the emergence of an essential self for which there can indeed be no precedent and for which, of course, there can be no guarantees of success in the future. The purpose of this book is indeed to offer a paradigm that can give sociological shape to the possibilities for genuine freedom and unfeigned solidarity in the most secular of societies.

1 *Origins of the Cult of Authority*

> A general spirit of revolt, such as I advocate here, is directed
> against the totality of an absurd civilization—against its
> ethos, its morality, its economy, and its political structure
> (Read, *Anarchy and Order*, p. 26).

(in the existential sense .)

READ'S CALL FOR A SPIRIT OF REVOLT asserts that our
civilization is absurd; it should therefore be ignored or abandoned
to make room for a new spirit with life-giving symbols. Of course,
civilization is potentially absurd, no matter how effectively it is
transmitted or faithfully it is acquired, because it manifestly offers
only ambiguous symbols of a life transcending death. In apparently opening the way to continuity and wholeness beyond
one's own lifetime, cultures covertly offer reminders of finitude
and death itself. Any symbol that appears to transcend death also
points however unwittingly, to death itself as an inevitable limit
on all human projects. Every reference to eternity reminds us of
mortality. That reminder is not lost, even on those who wish to
believe in one form of immortality or another. I am arguing that a
secularized culture then is particularly vulnerable, and all authority that derives from that culture is subject to "a general spirit of
revolt." X

Let us assume that a society's beliefs and values, its symbols
and sacred stories, all offer a way out of the impasse of death.
Lifton, for instance, makes such an assumption on psychoanalytic
grounds; humans need guarantees of their immortality and so
develop "culture by changing natural conditions in order to maintain [their] spiritual self" (1976, 1983:32, no. 4). Despite a widespread popular belief in life after death, however, one can argue
that Western culture is doing poorly in providing intimations of

21

immortality. Sometimes the fault is found with the institutions that are supposed to carry the culture but fail to exhibit and transmit crucial beliefs and values; so argues Lifton, who goes on to add that the twentieth century's list of disasters and catastrophes, from war and genocide to the atrophy and destruction of the natural environment have broken through cultural defenses against despair (1976, 1983:35). If Lifton is right, and I think he is, the authority of a secular culture, and with it the cult of authority, are increasingly susceptible to revolt.

Any revolt against culture will logically draw from the same deep wells as the revolt against death. Although in civilization humans have created a screen or shield against death, that cultural defense, however, becomes a burden and an impediment; it is difficult to carry because it also requires a sacrifice of certain impulses and strivings for life. Freud (1963:294–300) argued that the god of civilization is a jealous god indeed and requires certain sacrifices of instinct; civilization must be renewed constantly. Lifton also notes the fatal implications of a civilization that appears on the surface to be offering a way to life eternal. In referring to Otto Rank, he notes that life, experienced as a "loan" from an external source, must eventually be repaid; if accepted, the loan eventually must be paid in the form of a debt, which is death itself (1976, 1983:42). This sense of indebtedness derives from culture and reinforces the cult of authority. In a more secularized society, however, a culture that imposes such general, longstanding, and indefinite obligations will seem increasingly absurd.

In a sense, *any* civilization locates the source of life outside the individual in the agreeable and attractive form of a spiritual existence that transcends the limitations of the flesh and of a single lifetime. Lifton therefore duly notes Freud's point that all civilization provides a certain dulling and numbing of sensation. But Lifton argues that it is the *failure* of civilization, not its success, that causes individuals to despair and results in a listlessness of heart and spirit: the failure of civilization to provide forms and images that give order, meaning, direction, and hope to an individual's experiences. The reasons for the difference between Lifton and Freud need not detain us; Lifton acknowledges them in some detail in his discussion of the theory of instincts (1976; 1983, chapter 3, 49ff.). I am suggesting that in a secular society, civilization will fail to suppress vital impulses and will not be needed to give these impulses form and meaning.

A secular society, then, is intrinsically anxiety-producing because it attacks any symbols that become sacred and demand
various forms and degrees of human sacrifice, including death
itself. In a secular society, all social obligations are temporary,
even those that are "for life," since this life will end. Secularity
undermines the notion that life is a gift that in the end must be
returned to the giver and the source. Death is no longer a form of
payment of one's debt in society. At the most, it is a release from
all obligation.

To live in a secular society will therefore require an individual to
tolerate painful anxiety. Consider Lifton's description of the three
major issues that one must face in the early stages of life: issues
that one addresses later in life as it becomes increasingly apparent
in middle age that death will interrupt one's projects before some,
even many, of them are completed. To establish a sense of one's
own immortality, Lifton argues, one must have a sense of what
Erikson calls "basic trust" in the world, in others, and so eventually in one's own self. To achieve this sense of certainty that one's
life will endure requires "confidence in the integrity, connection,
and movement of life" (Lifton 1976, 1983:40). If Lifton is right, the
maturing individual also requires a sense of connection with
others by connecting "with the modes of symbolic immortality"
(ibid.:39). The same with integrity; one's sense of wholeness
comes through acquiring symbols that make sense of one's relationship to the world and to the future (ibid.:38). As for a sense of
movement, his argument also requires that the individual overcome stagnation through moving in a direction suggested by
symbols that stand for progress toward goals immune to the death
of the individual. I am arguing, however, that in a secular society,
connection and movement will come, if they come at all, not
through symbol or culture but through vital social organizations
and communities. Integrity, if it comes, will be purchased at the
price of considerable anxiety: the anxiety that comes from experiencing one's life as (only) one's own.

If a secular culture no longer requires one to make sacrifices as a
cure for one's anxiety over death and as a payment for the "gift" of
life, are individuals nonetheless duped by their social system?
That was the question that I raised in the introduction, and I
return to it here for the remainder of this chapter. The answer is a
simple but tentative "Yes." I have already argued that individuals
in a complex society are in a paradoxical situation. Employed in

large bureaucracies, they have an extraordinary impact on the lives of strangers, an impact that is pervasive, indirect, and therefore all the more difficult to assess. As their impact is enlarged, however, their obligations are narrowed. The requirements of particular jobs require individuals to be responsible only for their immediate duties: duties that are quite specific, on the whole, and subject to change. Given little substantive freedom and responsibility, they are nonetheless in a position to influence, even to devastate, the lives of thousands of their fellow citizens in the course of implementing social policies, producing toxic products, withholding benefits, or tightening requirements for eligibility to one program or another. The anxiety that would be created by direct social conflict is relieved by the ritualized procedures of their organizations. The sense of liability for the consequences of their actions is limited by their incorporation into large bodies that operate within (if not always according to) the law. The sense that one has done only a very little in the course of one's lifetime is subsumed under the awareness that the social structure outlives the individual; a spurious continuity is gained through the continuous operation of formal organizations that may have been lost in the culture itself. A social system of this sort offers protections against remorse and despair, protections no less effective for being part of a taken-for-granted social, rather than cultural, order.

Under these conditions, an individual's obligations remain secularized, although the social system takes on authority—the right to take final responsibility for the costs and sacrifices caused by the operation of the social system. If there is to be a wholly secularized society, of course, precisely that authority, the authority of the system per se, will have to be challenged. That authority is so difficult to challenge, that some sociologists have been eager to apply the term "sacred" to the system's major institutions, organizations, and ways of operating. Some would consider the judiciary and the Constitution themselves as sacred institutions (cf. Hammond 1974). Others find the sacred in the overwhelming power and scope of large corporations and bureaucracies (Shils 1975). Still others find the sacred enshrined in certain hallowed rules for governing social conflict, e.g., honesty, fair play, and the free exercise of individual will and ambition (cf. Herberg 1955; Williams 1970). Whether such use of the term "sacred" serves any clear analytical purpose is doubtful, but the use does serve the rhetorical purpose of pointing out certain obstacles to the process of secularization. In that sense, it might seem reasonable to speak here of the authority of a social system as a "sacred" barrier to the further development of a secular society.

To avoid the suggestion that the "sacred" is sacrosanct, however, I prefer to borrow Bakunin's phrase, the "cult of authority:"

> The proletariat of the great cities of France, and even of Paris, still cling to many Jacobin prejudices, and to many dictatorial and governmental concepts. The cult of authority—the fatal result of religious education, that historic source of all evils, deprivations, and servitude—has not yet been completely eradicated in them. This is so true that even the most intelligent children of the people, the most convinced socialists, have not freed themselves completely of these ideas. If you rummage around a bit in their minds, you will find the Jacobin, the advocate of government, cowering in a dark corner, humble but not quite dead. (Dolgoff 1972:266)

The tendency to ritualize social conflict by seeking resolution from a third party whose word is final is no doubt cultic, but like most cults, the tendency is unstable and amorphous. It is the capacity to have the last word, I suggest, that is the defining characteristic of authority. The extent to which that authority is open to challenge is the problem to which this chapter is addressed. It is a difficult problem precisely because this "cult of authority" is a ritualized expression of social conflict that takes many forms and no form in particular, and is evanescent. Nonetheless, the cult of authority is itself the primary barrier to a secular society.

Of course, in the semantics of the term "cult" lies embedded a theory. In unpacking the term, I intend to provide a brief sketch of the social problems that contribute to the demand for authority. There are problems partly in resolving conflict directly, with all the pain, freedom, and spontaneity that such immediate resolution requires. There are also problems in resolving conflict specifically rather than in transforming it into symbolic issues that are easier to discuss, manipulate and "resolve." Indeed, what often passes for "conflict resolution" is just the opposite of a resolution—the displacement of conflict from the scene of its origin to another locale, e.g., the courts; the transformation of conflict from the original issue to a related but more abstract or easily symbolized form; and the adjudication of the conflict in a form that, in fact, does not provide a final word but opens the way to a continuing process of negotiation. In a partially secularized society, of course, obligations may well be direct, immediate, and specific, while conflicts are resolved in ways that are highly abstract, indirect, and protracted. It is this asymmetry between obligations and the resolution of conflict that makes individuals "dupes" of the social system and underlies the tendency for authority itself to become cultic.

Keep in mind two points, if you will: that authority derives, in part, from the capacity to resolve social conflict; and that authority becomes cultic as the means for resolving social conflict become more ritualized. The first step in such ritualization is displacing social conflict from the place of origin to a separate social context and, in so doing, minimizing the pain of direct conflict. In this displacement, I suggest, lies one source of the cult of authority. In the second and third steps of ritualization the initial conflict becomes transformed into a symbol of some sort, like money or status, and enables the individual to identify with the authority that dispenses these symbolic awards. It is commonplace, of course, to locate the individual's unwillingness to challenge authority in a form of psychological resistance to anxiety. I locate this resistance in the individual's identification with authorities; once attacked, these authorities, in their internalized form, exact considerable emotional pain from the individual who ventures to attack them. The third stage in the process of ritualizing conflict accounts for the *persistence* of the individual's resistance to challenging authority; here the discussion focusses on the *secondary* psychological benefits of adhering to authorities. The benefits in question, of course, fall under the common heading of protecting the individual from various forms of anxiety such as feelings of helplessness, isolation, and remorse. In place of the pain of experiencing such emotions, I suggest the individual who has identified with—and subordinated himself or herself to—an authority, enjoys a derivative and grandiose feeling of self-importance. All of these reflections, I should add, are commonplace. Here they serve primarily to describe the support system for authority that goes beyond the most immediate and direct resolution of conflicts and ceases, therefore, to be temporary and occasional.

The general argument is that the cult of authority will only be weakened as conflict is increasingly less ritualized; as conflict is less ritualized, however, individuals will acquire a heavier burden of anxiety of the type that Lifton has described as contributing to "death-anxiety." Individuals will become increasingly unsure of their relationships as conflicts erode their sense of connection. With conflict also comes an increasing vulnerability and a threat to the individual's own boundaries of integrity. Conflict also threatens to reach an impasse or stalemate in which all forward movement ceases. Taken together, these contribute to the awareness that death itself may have the last word. It is not surprising, therefore, that individuals seek an authority whose word is final and so can deprive death of its sting.

Displacement

Violent class conflict is becoming less frequent in Western societies. Now, there are fewer dreams of proletarian glory, fewer violent uprisings, and correspondingly fewer periods of overt repression than in the late eighteenth and the nineteenth centuries. In the jargon of the social sciences, class conflict has become "institutionalized" (cf. Giddens 1982). This means that several developments appear to have become permanent. The first is the displacement of conflict from the streets to the bargaining table or to the courtroom. Here begins the development of ritualization in rules or formalities that need to be observed lest a fresh outbreak of violence occur in the wake of a breakdown of negotiations. These details of the law are often scrupulously observed and can impede as well as facilitate the resolution of the initial conflict. Ritualization continues to develop as bargaining focusses on symbolic rewards rather than on fundamental questions of power and authority. An entire conflict may be reduced to a discussion of cost-of-living increases or other benefits appropriately called "fringe" because they are not central to the fundamental conflict over class interests. With this stage in the ritualization of conflict, interests and differences become abstract rather than concrete. Debate focusses on problems in the industry, economic competition with foreign workers, a fair return on capital to investors, the rights of banks and other lenders, and abstract concepts of productivity. Left behind temporarily are the concrete problems and needs of particular individuals or groups. Eventually, the conflict resolved at the bargaining table will again surface as the issues take very concrete forms of suffering for particular workers whose plant is closed or whose jobs are declared redundant.

All decisions are as impersonal, of course, as the reasons given for them are abstract. Indeed, ritualization leads to a development that might be called *super-individuation*, since the interests of a particular person are seldom considered or made the issue of class

conflict. Conflict becomes, almost by definition, a matter of categories of workers rather than of individuals per se as they face
apparently abstract questions of productivity, investment, and
proper management. However, to the person who suffers the loss
of a job, becomes depressed, or is unable to find other work, those
sufferings call for meaning and redemption. Super-individuation
occurs as those losses make possible the gains of others and so
appear redemptive. In this way, individuals may gain stature and
dignity who nonetheless lose all hope for the relief or redress of
their own grievances.

Conversely, particular managers make decisions, e.g., whether
or not to modernize a plant. Those decisions make some workers
more vulnerable than others; indeed an entire plant and a surrounding community may be stifled or damaged beyond repair.
Nonetheless, the management's decisions are *supra*-individual,
and no individuals are held responsible for negligence, let alone
for manslaughter, when particular workers suffer and perhaps die
as a result of those management "practices." The process of
ritualizing class conflict thus may result in a cult of authority in
which the victims become heroic in their suffering and the social
system becomes increasingly abstract, impersonal, and even
"ghostly." I am suggesting that to ritualize conflict in this way can
become obsessive; to that extent the appeal to authority becomes
cultic. In any event, the first step is displacement. Just as the
obsessive goes through rituals in order to prevent something
awful from happening and seeks in that process to avoid being
disturbed, the ritualization of class conflict begins by displacing
fights to the courtroom or to the bargaining table where disturbance can be minimized and mortal injuries avoided.

Note the loss of individual autonomy and self-determination
that accompanies the ritualization of conflict. Once displaced,
conflict goes underground and emerges on the surface of social
life in a different form. Freud's characters, whether drawn from
case studies or from well-known fictional characters, frequently
disguise their emotional conflict by claiming to be helpless. It is
this passivity and helplessness, the despair and hopelessness that
discouraged even the most ardent anarchists in their attempts to
focus industrial conflict at its source. Bukanin and Goldmann are
particularly outspoken about the chronic helplessness of the mass
of people who seem to prefer their own sufferings to any social life
that could provide less punishment. My point is simply that, by

displacing class conflict and all its violence to a more secure setting, such as the bargaining table, the workers' movement practically guaranteed that such conflict would go underground and emerge in the disguise of issues like low productivity or other ways that workers express both their desire to cheat those who have deprived them of their rightful rewards and also cheat themselves by accepting less than what is rightfully owed them.

After conflict has been displaced, workers, having been cheated of control, will repress their anger. This anger remains repressed, sometimes finding expression in imaginery acts of murder, for which they expiate their resulting guilt by suffering various disabilities.

A Case of Social Pathology: Ritualized Conflict in West Virginia

In his study of mine workers in West Virginia, Kai Erikson (1976) provides us with a telling account of the several steps in the process by which suffering is displaced and conflict begins to be ritualized. In *Everything in Its Path*, he recounts how an Appalachian community was destroyed as a dam, made of waste from local mines, collapsed and released millions of tons of sludge and water on people trapped in a mining valley along Buffalo Creek. It was the final stage of conflict between workers and management in that mining valley. Erikson notes that earlier uprisings of mine workers had been fully as violent as any clash between workers and owners in this country or in Europe. A pitched battle was fought with bombs and machine guns. Workers marched from the north to join workers in the south. But the mine owners won that battle, and the subsequent repression was swift and brutal. Workers thought to be sympathetic to the union were beaten and fired. The remaining workers were pacified by welfare, patronized by the local authorities, kept hopelessly in debt by the system of scriptmoney and credit at the company store. There were ceaseless reminders of what the workers owed the company; the symbols of everyday life reminded them of a debt that they must someday pay—if they should live so long.

As the miners lost their capacity for autonomy and their ability to resolve their disputes with the company, class conflict was displaced from open battles into a protracted struggle for symbols. The struggle for symbols not only disguised the nature of the real conflict but reinforced the guilt of those miners who secretly yearned to eliminate the repressive force of a company whose demands so often proved fatal. Along Buffalo Creek, black lung disease, falling slate, sheer exhaustion, and the quiet sickness of despair were, indeed, fatal, decreed by a fate that resided in the offices of the company. So begins the "cult" of authority. As conflict is displaced to other areas, disturbances decrease, but individuals become more chronically, if unconsciously disturbed, and the nature of the real conflict is disguised as a contest for the *symbols* of individuation, e.g., money, status, dignity.

Besides "formalities" and the routines of management and union, other ceremonials softened conflict in that mining valley. Erikson notes how simple greetings and gestures among friends and neighbors carried a world of meaning. One simply knew that the community was there to help and sustain; the prescribed gestures said as much. Like any formalities, they permitted individuals to take a few liberties: for instance, to help themselves to coffee in each other's kitchens, or to inquire in the night why the neighbor's light was still burning. Few could give a formal and abstract account of these proceedings; the workers were not versed in sociological reasoning. But they had their own abstractions for the way things were; Erikson simply called it their tradition. It was a mixture of memories and assumptions that required little explanation but made sense of the world in which they lived, memories of what their fathers and mothers had done, and assumptions about what it meant to be a man or a woman, a neighbor and a friend. Had these assumptions been more clearly stated, they might have been more easily tested, revised, and updated in time to prevent the disaster or, even afterwards, in time to develop new patterns for living together and new reasons for being. Unstated as they were, the abstractions took on enough sanctity to remain unexamined and persistent. If there were an early tendency toward super-individuation, it may well be that the workers and their families thought of themselves as saints and sinners, caught up in a cosmic drama in which their sufferings had redemptive significance. Once they had been "lost," but now were "found," over and over again, of course, in the spasmodic revivals of religious enthusiasm that brought them fresh experiences of guilt and forgiveness, spiritual redemption and release. Their selves were "super" in another sense. Because they were so wrapped up in the vestments of identity provided by the community, their place in the community gave them a super-identity that merged with specific people (a father, a mother, a more distant ancestor), and with specific things (a watch handed from father to son), or a specific place (this homesite, this valley). Taking away these momentoes and landmarks would mean a loss of that super-individual self. In the flood, of course, that was precisely what was stripped away. The remaining identity, too fragile and too suddenly deprived of protection, took a long time to feel alive and able again to cope with life, and also with death.

From Symbolizing Conflict to Identifying with Authority

In a post-Freudian era, however, we have come to understand that those who seek to overthrow the chief authority of any society are committing the political crime of parricide. The punishment for lèse-majesté, as Freud also called it, must fit the crime; *lex talionis* requires an eye for an eye, a tooth for a tooth. The unconscious, like the state, is often literal minded; it substitutes bodily parts for moral principles. The state may seek to sever the heads from the bodies of those who attack the highest authorities; the unconscious also reinforces the cult of authority in the self-inflicted punishment of radicals or rebels who become, as Freud put it of Dostoyevsky and his "seizures," victims of a cruel conscience who act out in their own bodies the dread of punishment and its effects. Some, like Dostoyevsky go into spasms; others enjoy protracted stagnation and inhibition. Those who overthrow the heads of state, therefore, yield willingly to the revenge of the authorities. As Bakunin reminds us, the French authorities indeed were extraordinarily brutal in their vengeance toward members of the Commune of Paris.

It is as if the child, having slain the father, desires to be scourged by the father's ghost; long periods of inhibition and low productivity may act out the death that the child *wanted* to inflict on the parents. Some, like Dostoyevsky, who want to be loved by the same father whom they hated and eliminated, if only in spirit, become passive and willingly accept renewed affliction as a punishment that seems like a token of their father's love. Religion sometimes reminds us, after all, that the Lord chastens those whom He loves, a clear invitation to wholesale masochism. That invitation was no doubt taken up by vast numbers of Russian peasants who, still mystified by the alliance of the state with religion, had a sanctified affection for the authorities whom they had at least momentarily displaced from their thrones. No wonder so many seemed passive, helpless, and willing to endure awful deprivation in the years following the brief uprisings of the nineteenth century.

In examining this alternation between periods of liberation and renewed servitude, Freud (1963:284) writes of Dostoyevsky:

> His early symptom of death-like seizures can thus be understood as a father-identification on the part of his ego, permitted by his superego as punishment. "You wanted to kill your father in order to be your father yourself. Now you *are* your father, but a dead father"—the regular mechanism of hysterical symptoms. And further: "Now your father is killing *you*."

Of the miners and their families studied by Erikson, many felt that the managers of the mining company, Pittson, were guilty of filicide, the crime of killing one's child. Although Erikson does not explictly interpret this as a confession, it is clear that for years the workers have thought of the company as children would a father—a provider of sorts, but also a powerful figure who, like the father in the unconscious, exacts a terrible penalty from those who might rebel and seek to take possession of the prize. Erikson tells us clearly that workers thought of the mines and their valuable secrets as a source of nourishment like mother earth; they even sucked on coal as though it were candy (or even a nipple?). Had the workers entertained any secret desires to overthrow the patriarchal authority of the company, they might well have felt that they also deserved their eventual punishment. No wonder that so many of them failed to take precautions and prevent the disaster. As Freud reminds us, *fate* is often the symbol for the father's insuperable authority. It is as if the symbols of conflict expressed what the unconscious rebel secretly knows: that the rebel has a debt to pay to the same authority he would have gladly cheated of its power. The parricide's guilt, as Freud said of Dostoyevsky, is easily transformed in the rebel's mind into a debt that must be paid.

Let us return to Freud. In the passage I quoted, in which Freud speaks of Dostoyevsky's guilt-ridden seizures, he goes on to note:

> One thing is remarkable: in the aura of the epileptic attack, one moment of supreme bliss is experienced. This may very well be a record of the triumph and sense of liberation felt on hearing the news of the death [of the father], to be followed immediately by an all the more cruel punishment. We have divined just such a se-

quence of triumph and mourning, of festive joy and mourning, in the brothers of the primal horde who murdered their father, and we find it repeated in the ceremony of the totem meal. (1963:284)

Certainly the class conflicts of the nineteenth century did not last for long. In each case, the triumphant revolutionaries became victims of reprisals by the state, reprisals, as Bakunin (1972:266) pointed out, that were not entirely unwelcome to some socialists. Indeed, from his description of the revolt of the Paris Commu-nards, it appeared that the population waited in quiet expectation of the troops' return and the government's revenge.

In making themselves more than mere individuals but embodi-ments of some social purpose, common value, or sacred memory, individuals do more than cover up their underlying self-hatred; they live in a dream world in which not only they, but those who govern them, are superb. The anarchist manifestoes know that this is where the cult of authority takes deeper root, in the hunger of individuals to stand tall, indeed, taller than average, and to find in themselves the significance that they desperately seek for their lives. Of course the workers of Buffalo Creek considered their company's managers to be paternal authorities not only because of some "cultural lag" that confused the head of the family with the head of the company, not only because they wished to avoid the terror of being under the control of those who do not care, but also because they hungered for that larger significance that can come from being identified with the powerful and significant. Kropotkin does not call this hunger for being more-than-ordinary either superbia or narcissism, but he describes it very well:

> Ah, if men were those superior beings that the utopians of authority like to speak to us of, if we could close our eyes to reality and live like them in the world of dreams and illusions as to the superiority of those who think themselves called to power, perhaps we should also do like them; perhaps we also should believe in the virtues of those who govern. . . . The employer would never be the tyrant of the worker; he would be the father! The factory would be a palace of delight, and never would masses of workers be doomed to physical deterioration. (1927, 1970:135–36)

Kropotkin clearly is speaking here of a cult of god-like figures. He warns against thinking of those who govern as a caste apart, composed of those without "knowledge of simple mortals' weak-nesses" (1927; 1970: 136). The point, however, is even sharper than the use of such words as "utopia" or "cult" might suggest. Kropotkin is talking about a net loss of an individual's grasp of reality; "we know men too well to dream such dreams" (ibid.:136). This knowledge, however, leads to an awareness of one's own corruptibility—the anarchist harbors no illusions about anyone's goodness or reliability. If those in authority are no more altruistic or dependable than the individual himself, the individual is deprived of another psychic protection against the loss of integrity and against death itself.

There is another hint in Kropotkin about the nature of these god-like creatures who stand between the individual and a grasp of reality. Listen again to the last phrase in the passage quoted above. The employer, if he were like a father, would turn the factory into a "palace of delight": a harem perhaps, a place where pleasure knows no bounds. The worst enemy of the worker is ultimately a dream in which the gods not only govern but copulate at will; they turn the factory into a palace of delight where one can enjoy certain (unnamed) pleasures. This is the god, then, who along with the harsh tyrant, authority itself, keeps demanding sacrifices and makes continued claims on the worker. To put it another way, if workers unconsciously believe that they are cheating on some authority, if guilt holds the worker down, who then is the tyrant who keeps life from being free and pleasurable? It is not only the factory owner who owes the worker a living and deprives the worker of the pleasures of life. That god resides in the heart of the worker and feels perennially cheated of what is rightfully his or her pleasure.

We can now understand why Kropotkin says that the individual is merely mortal and wholly corruptible (1927, 1970:136). Of course power corrupts; there is, however, no doubt that the worker would gladly turn the tables not only on the authoritarian tyrant but on the employer who monopolizes pleasure and has the "droit de seigneur." But true freedom requires that the individual renounce such power and, with it, the authority of the internal god who feels chronically cheated of certain pleasures. The individual who would be free must renounce all demands for heaven on earth, for unlimited pleasures, for license, in every sense of that word. Only by such self-education, impossible to those whose pleasures are taken from them or else scarcely permitted by external authorites, will workers and citizens learn to live peaceably together. Under the regime of their own authority, individuals will no longer be burdened by the guilt they feel for having cheated a jealous god of what that god deems its rightful satisfaction.

A passage in Freud explains how the cult of authority stems from the wish for license to enjoy the pleasures of gods.

> Speaking in analytical terms, we should say that the instinctual life, the id, is the god who is defrauded when the gratification of extinguishing fires (by satisfying the flames of passion) is renounced: a human desire is transformed in the legend into a divine privilege. But the divinity in the story has nothing of the character of a super-ego: it is still the representative of the paramount instinctual life (1963:296).

Prometheus steals from the gods their control over the pleasures and passions; he is therefore doomed to recurring cycles of pleasure and decay. It is only in the dream world fostered by the cult of authority that workers will be saved by their "gods," by their "authorities," from "physical deterioration." Once they know that there is no Utopia, that no factory will ever be a palace of delight (i.e., when workers give up their worship of the gods and renounce their unlimited desires for unlimited pleasures), only then will the cult of authority be finished. On that day, of course, workers will have to come to terms with their own mortality, their eventual "physical deterioration," and their inevitable death.

Coda

In a partially secularized society, it is too late to suggest that authority takes the vivid, concrete form of the sacred in highly visible and impressive symbols and institutions. It makes more sense to speak of "a cult" of authority, an approach to agencies and individuals who can offer the final word in various forms of social conflict. That approach is ritualized, although it may never again take the form of a highly developed and sacred ritual.

There are several steps in the ritualization of social conflict, each of which contributes to the cultic development of social authority. The first step is simply to displace conflict from its place of origin to a "demilitarized" zone, so to speak; there certain formalities can be observed, a proper ceremonial, the immediate purpose of which is to avoid the outbreak of actual hostilities. The second step is to transform the real substance of the conflict into a symbol e.g. money that can take the place of blood or other forms of payment for damages incurred in the conflict. To substitute symbols for actual sacrifice ritualizes conflict by contributing to the authority of whatever agency can pass sentence, resolve a dispute, and exact symbolic payment from the adversaries. Other steps in the ritualization of conflict follow from these first two. As the substance of the conflict becomes more symbolic, the bases of authority become increasingly impersonal and abstract, transcending the conflict. As authority becomes increasingly abstract and impersonal, individuals find that their own personal interests become subsumed under categories, a further step in ritualization of conflict. As individuals become incorporated into a class, or transformed into a particular instance or "case" of a more general phenomenon, the bases of authority become even more abstract. Indeed, they become enviable. Individuals who therefore identify themselves with such authorites take on, in their own minds, both the transcendence of these figures and the force of their judgments; so are laid the bases of the individual's own grandiosity and self-hatred. In such self-abasement and self-expansion the ritualization of conflict leads even further to the cultic development of social authority. In this way, the cult of authority originates and develops the psychological bases for resistance to attacks on the authority in question. I have based this brief sketch on materials drawn from the sociological analysis of social conflict in specific communities as well as from some sources in the psychoanalytic literature, and the discussion is essentially schematic. Its purpose is to set out some commonplace notions on which to develop a picture of authority in a partially secularized society. We can then infer the bases of authority in a society that is so highly secularized as to have only the most contingent forms of social obligation.

It may also help to briefly review the reasons I have given for regarding American society as only partially secularized. On the one hand, the culture (what Read calls "ethos" and "morality") does not offer the sure and certain sources of triumph over death that a more highly integrated and sacred set of symbols can proclaim. American culture, of course, is a mixture of symbols that taps the roots of ancient collective experience and also offers only the most abstract and impersonal values, like fairness and efficiency on which to base a lifetime of effort and by which to legitimate the sacrifices called for by the society itself. American culture provides *indirect* reminders of the mortality that it seeks to transcend, but because the culture is abstract, complex, pluralistic, and poorly integrated, it fails wholly to legitimate sacrifices and provide guarantees of meaning. No longer "duped" by the culture, individuals still have to contend with a social system that does offer a sense of connection and continuity: connection with individuals in distant markets and in a variety of audiences or locales; continuity of effort and administration, if not of direction and policy, long after the particular individual is dead.

The culture may fail to legitimate an individual's sacrifices, but the lack of meaning does not present a crisis so long as the social system begs the question of personal responsibility for actions that have a potent effect on a wide range of people. A complex and highly bureaucratized society seeks to avoid asking the questions that the culture cannot satisfactorily answer. Where the culture fails, moreover, to provide a sense of scope and continuity to individual effort beyond the circumstances of a particular lifetime, the social system, by its very imperturbability, offers the appearance of transcendence. Like a ritual performed to avoid a profound disturbance, the system goes on.

Our set of commonplaces, however, is not complete until we discuss individuals in themselves, not merely as carriers of a culture or as participants in more or less ritualized forms of social conflict, but as persons with minds and imaginations that only dimly reflect and may profoundly distort their social environment. As a sociologist, I am obliged to complete any analytical scheme by a reference not only to "culture" and "society," but to "personality." The personality, however, lies partly inside and partly outside any social system. Parts of a society become deeply imbedded in the self, and parts of the self firmly resist all such intrusions until the very end. What shall we include, then, of the individual—as a separate person so to speak—in this initial scheme for outlining the general shape and scope of a secular society?

Three simple axioms can serve as an introduction to the next section of the chapter. One, a society may be far more—or far less—secular than the individuals in it. From a society's pattern of obligation and authority one cannot infer much about the individuals who make up that system, just as one cannot generalize to a whole society no matter how many individuals one includes in one's sample. The two levels are analytically and empirically discrete. The second axiom follows from the first: that individuals may represent a built-in limit to how secularized a society may become. That point is a truism, since there is no simple way to verify or refute it. Once stated, however, that axiom opens the way to a third: that so long as there is asymmetry in the extent to which a society and its individuals are secularized, the process of secularization is reversible.

THE PARTIALLY SECULARIZED SELF

It is easy to see wherein lies the resemblance between neurotic ceremonial and religious rites; it is in the fear of pangs of conscience after their omission, in the complete isolation of them from all other activities (the feeling that one must not be disturbed) and in the conscientiousness with which the details are carried out (Freud, 1963:19).

Clearly ceremonial (neurotic or otherwise) originates in a desire, as Freud put it, not to be "disturbed," to avoid painful emotions. In the next passage, Freud gives us several examples of patients who went through odd maneuvers to prevent painful reminiscences from disturbing their thoughts, and in each case the source of their pain is the same. It is separation, a parting. In one case, it is a young woman who is attempting to preserve a union between her married sister and that sister's husband; in another case, it is a woman reenacting moments in which she and her husband either failed to come together or actually parted. It is clear from these case histories that the anxiety and pain of separation impel some people to take extraordinary precautions. In these precautions, we can discern the origins of social life in the ritualization of conflict and a profound desire to be rescued from or to prevent an anxiety that, once it becomes a way of life, constitutes chronic death-anxiety.

We can now understand more profoundly why the ritualization of conflict shifts away from direct memory and experience, painful as it is, to something tangential, related symbolically or only by circumstance to the initial experience. The details of neurotic performances only seem trivial, Freud notes, if one fails to understand their inner connection to memory and feelings seeking to come up from the unconscious. To avoid what is coming up from below, so to speak, the mind moves sideways to something that lies readily at hand. The precautions then focus on the details, superfluous as they are. In a religious ritual, of course, extraordinary precautions against a faulty performance often do focus precisely on minor matters, such as the arrangements of cloth and candles and the choice of particular gestures or other accompaniments. These are mere accompaniments, however, and not the thing itself. They are a mere distraction from the original source of anxiety.

Even these distracting defenses, Freud notes, cannot fail to become transparent, and so in some way reveal their origins. The truth will come out, no matter how disguised in liturgical or neurotic minutiae. Priests must gather up the crumbs of the consecrated bread that nothing be wasted; yet it is precisely a life that was destroyed or "wasted," as modern slang puts it, that the ritual seeks to recall. If not done properly, the ritual of the Eucharist will fail to forestall other crucifixions, and the reign of love will be further delayed. In fact, some preambles to the celebration of the Eucharist do warn of dire misfortunes that may fall upon those who come inadequately prepared to the rite. The original anxiety is to avoid a painful separation, and the Eucharist involves a symbolic fracture of the bread; thus, the participants recall a time when the tie between God and man was nearly broken by violent hatred. Only the proper performance of the rite can help to heal that awful breach. Like culture, neurotic and religious ceremonies provide reminders of what they appear to have transcended, e.g., separation, loss, and death itself. No doubt individuals will remember what a culture or a society seeks to forget.

As long as conflict is thus ritualized, even in everyday life, rather than in neurotic ceremony or religious rite, individuals will seek authoriative protection, and readily consent to be dominated by the right way of doing things. Domination comes to them, therefore, in the apparently benign form of protection. As Freud put it, "a ceremonial begins as an act of defence or security—*a protective measure*" (1963:23). It is precisely the claim made by anarchists, that repressive social order comes initially from the search of minorities and threatened groups for protection against painful deprivations and losses. In their search for protection, however, deprived minorities turn to the "authorities," as they turned in the twelfth and thirteenth centuries to lords, princes, and the Church itself. In so doing, these groups surrendered their autonomy for a measure of protection, just as the individual, compelled to engage in the ceremonial of obsession, loses control over his or her own destiny. Individuals and groups thus abandon themselves to certain formulae, rites, and to the protection of superior powers. What religion calls self-abandonment appears to this observer merely as self-estrangement. The question is whether the capacity for such self-estrangement sets limits on the process of secularization.

Why groups should turn to protectors who then punish them with a severe discipline is no more obvious than why individuals should seek to repeat obsessive actions in search of relief and absolution. Freud argues, however, that normal and compulsive ritual is often the result of a sense of guilt that "has its origin in certain early psychological occurrences" (1963:32). Those occurrences, I would add, are a series of separations over which the child has no control, as parents and other caretakers come and go of their own free will. In these separations arise the child's initial experience of anxiety and even panic. Enough is known of the magical aspects of infantile thinking, however, to suggest that the child seeks to control anxiety by exercising magical control, at least in his own mind, over the individuals who otherwise seem to leave for no good reason and to return when they wish. In the magical world of childhood, the child's wish seems to generate the reappearance of the parents. It is not difficult for the child to believe that another wish accounts for their disappearance. From this assumption, it is understandable that the child feels responsible, and therefore guilty, for appearances and separations over which the child, *in fact*, has *no* control. Extended into adulthood, however, such guilt may inspire the wish to reverse the process of secularization in order to return, as it were, to the "faith of the fathers" and mothers.

The wish to exercise such power stems from the underlying anxiety caused by helplessness in the face of separation. The wish intensifies when the child meets individuals whose presence is abhorrent, such as siblings, and parents whose presence may at times be painful, as in the case of parents who insist on rigorous toilet training or other painful proceedings. Under these conditions, magical thoughts give the child's wishes for companionship and mastery a potency that can generate a sense of guilt. That guilty sensibility lasts, in some cases, a lifetime and calls for repeated cleansings and absolutions. Ceremonials, however, may reinforce and intensify the anguish they are intended to relieve. Ritualized forms of social life protect the individual from panic and anxiety, by expressing magical wishes and offering imaginary controls that also intensify the fear of a breach in these predictable and customary performances and prolong the search for protection from powerful figures. The more smoothly a society's institutions adjudicate conflict, the more dependent and the more reverent individuals may become. Beneath the surface of rational procedures, then, may be attitudes that are all too ready to abandon control to powerful and dependable authorities.

In anarchist criticism of the law, all legislation, like an obsessive ritual, separates us from our original state of spontaneity and from our destiny, which is to be free and self-determining. In fact, even the best laws simply restore the privileges once enjoyed by medieval cities before they were dominated by nobles and kings (Kropotkin 1927, 1970:211). These laws have made us accustomed to being dominated by a system that serves other than our own best interests, and through the law we have come to accept and approve the "right of society *to punish*" (Kropotkin 1927, 1970:215). The law provides a spurious order rather than the harmony that would emerge if individuals settled their own quarrels rather than helplessly seeking protection from those to whom they delegate the right to punish. Under the auspices of the state, individuals grow up to accept the state's authority to punish as well as to protect, as though that were the natural order of things. As Freud noted, ceremonials of an obsessive sort betray their pathological origin by serving to ward off a punishment that the individual feels is both inevitable and richly deserved. In the absence of such a punitive function, the ceremonial might be simply trivial or purely an aesthetic and playful elaboration of childhood tendencies.

If a secularizing society is to proceed and further reduce both social obligation and social authority, the problems of unconscious guilt will have to be solved. I have mentioned some of the sources of such guilt in childhood fantasies of omnipotence and in magical thinking, and we started this chapter with references to the guilt of the individual for surviving others and for living, as it were, at others' expense. These are the residues of narcissism and they make their own contribution to the burden of unconscious guilt. There is still another source: the desire to commit murder that, Freud argues, inhabits every unconscious mind and, at least among the primitives, every conscious thought about the stranger and the enemy (1963:126 ff.). In all these ways, the Promethean egoist who seeks to satisfy all desires eliminates, at least in the world of dreams and magical thinking, all those who stand in the way of such satisfaction. Every child therefore grows up with the unremembered fantasies of having eliminated not only mere strangers, but those in the immediate family who barred the child from love. Underground, those memories become, as it were, "realistic," and the fantasies seem literally to have been true. Unconscious guilt is therefore the legacy of every childhood. The egoistic drives of all adults therefore call for continual restraint; that is the function of the law. The same drives expose the individual to constant temptations to commit, if only in fantasy, heinous crimes in order to gain loves that otherwise would be lost or denied. It is not only the neurotic who fears that something terrible is about to happen unless, of course, one performs preventive rituals in the right way. Egoistic drives tempt every individual to enjoy imaginary or unconscious murders even in the most advanced societies; no wonder, Freud might have said, that those societies become so formal, routine, impersonal, and complex that even bureaucracies take on the atmosphere and solemnity of a ritual. Ultimately, a secular society will require individuals to achieve some victories over narcissism and the magical thinking of childhood.

Conclusion

Both the anarchists and Freud are saying that more solidarity is needed to bind the hostile impulses that lead some to callous murder and others to more routine cruelties. Freud is very clear that in the mind of the most devoted spouse or child, there lurk hostile impulses as savage and primitive as any that troubled the soul of the tribesman: "With the exception of only a very few situations, there adheres to the tenderest and closest of our affections a vestige of hostility that can excite an unconscious death-wish" (1963:132). Freud, like the anarchists, found that the future would provide only a bleak scenario of increasing violence unless solidarity, warmhearted ties in which love binds hatred to itself, could provide new sources of unity and new barriers to the acting-out of murderous or vengeful impulses. Freud thought, as late as 1932, that the increasing unity of nations would forestall war, not only because of possible prohibitions against military actions, but because of "the growth of emotional ties between the members of a united group of people—feelings of unity which are the true source of its strength" (1963:137). Kropotkin could not agree more, but he might have placed his hopes in an international community of working people rather than in a transnational league of nation-states.

Under certain conditions, Kropotkin urged us to consider, conflict does not lead to the impasse that requires ritual and the continuous doing and undoing associated with social as well as with religious or neurotic rites. In discussing the medieval city, Kropotkin found there the seeds of international law (1970:230). When a city had a conflict with another city or a quarrel arose between competing guilds, the city would "send someone to 'seek the sentence' in a neighboring city" and to use arbitration, through the good offices of a third party, rather than surrender sovereignty over the matter to some external source of law and authority. *The capacity to provide the sentence that concludes a conflict to the satisfaction of both parties eliminates the need for ritualization.*

Sentencing is still just that: the authoritative speech that puts an end to a particular controversy. As the cities found themselves able to arbitrate their conflicts among themselves and to reach solutions that would be supported by local public opinion, so also did the guilds who had their own "international congresses of trades" (1970:230). Only when the guilds and cities refused to admit conflict and so created a situation in which one party would seek outside support for imposing a resolution did the authority of the Church and State prosper at the expense of the local cities and communes (1970:234-35). Where there is conflict among relatively equal partners who are tied together in solidarity as well as in competitive relationships, and where such conflict is resolved autonomously among the concerned parties (with or without a neutral third party), under these conditions violence is more likely to be avoided and freedoms to remain intact; in any event, authority is more likely to be local, indigenous, and functionally specific rather than external, expansive, and cultic.

As Kropotkin (1970:236–39) observed, it was primarily in the countryside that the state, through monarchy and other feudal institutions, developed its authority and exercised its force. Authority became sacred only to the extent that it imposed sentences rather than allowed sentences to emerge from the conversation of equal partners and parties to the conflict. Where the ties of solidarity that linked towns to one another and to the landed barons were not strong enough to contain the hostilities among them, and where the relationships of the peasants and the towns to the barons were too imbalanced to make the contestants fairly equal, "man fell in love with authority" (1970:240). That is why the anarchists called for an end to the "cult of authority" in general and of the state in particular: without these social defenses, groups, communities, and individuals will find it necessary to identify and to resolve their own conflicts. The removal, particularly of the state, is a necessary, if not sufficient, condition for the emergence of a wholly secular society.

There is no room in a fully secularized society for any sovereignty above the level at which individuals or communities, in cooperation or conflict with one another, directly exercise control over themselves. No authority may be delegated to a level at which it becomes independent and opposed to the will of the people; least of all should the state receive such delegations as permit it to claim sovereignty. Read quotes with approval a statement, made about the Russian state, that he would apply in principle to a wide variety of other, more overtly "democratic" states, viz. that the state had been "ruthlessly driving the nation everywhere, to its own formula of living," without any regard to differences among individuals or groups (1963:78). The problem is not just that the state overrides the will and opinion of the people it claims to represent, but that in turn the people lift the state to the level of a principle that is universal. "Sovereignty," as Read put it, is the "political religion" of modern societies (1954:134–35). No wonder, then, that such sovereignty has no place in a secular society.

2 The Chief Obstacle to a Secular Society: The Desire for a Common Fate

IN THIS CHAPTER, I will ask more about the type of character who can help to create a fully secular society. Such individuals will overturn institutions, attack the state, and liberate their own followers. If they are to help create a fully secular society, of course, they will need a strange combination of characteristics: an absence of crippling guilt and passivity, along with a realistic rather than grandiose self-image. They will avoid the tendency, on the one hand, toward sinful self-assertion; and, on the other, they will overcome the tendency to seek a unity with powerful figures and to submerse oneself in the sea of a common humanity. As a way of describing the problem of character we will look first, then, at the anarchists' demand for heroism. I will draw on psychoanalytic and theological discussions to define the type of character that can undertake to engage in social conflict without participating in or contributing to the cult of authority.

In a few lines, Emma Goldmann leaves no doubt that anarchism calls for heroic individuals; the fainthearted need not apply. Consider this description in which she calls for men (sic) to have the courage of their convictions:

> Anarchism therefore stands for direct action, the open defiance of, and resistance to, all laws and restrictions, economic, social, and moral. But defiance and resistance are illegal. Therein lies the salvation of men. Everything illegal necessitates integrity, self-reliance, and courage. In short, it calls for free, independent spirits, for "men who are *men*, and who have a bone in their backs which you cannot pass your hand through."
>
> Direct action, having proven effective along economic lines, is equally potent in the environment of the individual. There a hundred forces encroach upon his being, and only persistent resistance

45

to them will finally set him free. Direct action against the authority in the shop, direct action against the authority of the law, direct action against the invasive, meddlesome authority of our moral code, is the logical, consistent method of Anarchism (1969:65–66).

Clearly, we are here in the path of the saints and martyrs, of individuals who thought that the Sabbath (and all other institutions) were made for humans, and who took no thought for the morrow, since a daily encounter with evil would be more than enough challenge in itself. Goldmann writes in a long (and often Christian) tradition of antinomian witnesses and martyrs who refused to ritualize conflict and who therefore subverted the cult of authority.

There is also some respect for the person of iron will in much of anarchist thought: the egoist, the entrepreneur, the man of power who incarnates will. That is why Emma Goldmann scorns the working class, who "always follow like sheep led to the slaughter"; she prefers the dramatic figure of the capitalist who dominates and fights with a ruthless determination to preserve his power over labor (1969:262–63). When power is naked, the shape of the enemy is easily seen, and one can gird one's own loins for the task of rebellion. When conflict is direct rather than ritualized, there is less opportunity to romanticize either oneself or the enemy.

Unlike Emma Goldmann, however, other anarchists have been suspicious of their own hunger for heroic individuals who will raise the masses from their sheep-like preoccupations and confront the bureaucrats, soldiers, politicians, capitalists and clergy that dominate modern social systems. Herbert Read, as we have already seen, agrees that nothing less than a rebellion in every corner of society will begin to create the conditions hospitable to liberty and the creative imagination; he calls for (to quote him once again) "A general spirit of revolt . . . against the totality of an absurd civilization . . . against the method, its morality, its economy, and its political structure" (1954:26). Like Goldman, he not only calls for the overthrow of every institution, every encrusted privilege or habitual way of doing things; he also, like Goldmann, seeks to conjure up a genius, a poet, any hero indeed who will "recover a vision of the future and a spirit of revolt against the present" (1954:26). In an earlier essay, however, Read had objected to the fascist fascination with individuals of special talent and extraordinary achievement; he objected particularly to the fascist assumption that such heroic strides can be taken only as the result of individual genius rather than as the result of general social forces (1941, in 1963:52). Even the ability to make "good design," to make things with a fine aesthetic sense of proportion and usefulness, is a talent that calls far less for specific talent, he argued, than for a society that satisfies basic needs, and enables individuals to help one another in working toward common goals (1963:80). If the imagination is stultified, or the heart and will weak, blame such dispirited souls, he would argue, on bullying schoolmasters and ugly streets, on experts and politicians, on the weight of central planning and the stupefying effects of routine. It may take individuals of extraordinary courage to sound the prophetic message of anarchy; it will take individuals of equal courage and imagination to engage in actual battles in every bureaucratic nook and official cranny of a modern society. Read found the greatest hope, however, not in genius, but in talents and courage that are already "innate": the task is to find human beings that are "unspoilt" rather than extraordinarily gifted (1963:72). I am arguing that, if individuals are to avoid ritualizing social conflict, they will require the support of solidary groups and communities rather than the lonely heroism of the extraordinary messenger who stands alone. Prophecy is the calling of the people to come fully to their senses, but there must be a people, rather than a mass of solitary individuals, ready to be called.

The emergence of the anarchistic individual requires a psychological revolution. First, the individual must break ties with all those customs and people, all those institutions and authorities, that have given the individual a twofold sense of connectedness and power. In one of his most telling passages, Read argues that the anarchist must overcome any tendency to unite followers with leaders, a tendency so powerfully at work in Nazism. The fascist tendencies in anarchist thought, i.e., the appeal to extraordinary individuals with the will to lead otherwise inert and helpless masses, were clearly a danger, and Read understands very well the extent to which anarchist thought could give aid and comfort to fascist leaders. The glorification of the individual, combined with a scorn of the masses, can lead to sheer egoism on the one hand or to fascist leadership, on the other, so long as the cult of authority persists.

Read's warnings against the authoritarian or fascist streaks in anarchist thought depend heavily on the work of Fromm in *Escape from Freedom*. Two things impressed Read (1963:52–53) about Fromm's analysis of the individual. One was Fromm's accent on the individual's fear of being alone; the other was the emphasis Fromm placed on the individual's feelings of helplessness and craving for power. By fusing oneself in the imagination with another person, the individual, according to Fromm, achieves a feeling of oneness, of connection, that relieves the chronic and sometimes terrible anxiety of being alone. By feeling fused, if again only in the imagination, with a figure that seems powerful, the individual can also overcome feelings of helplessness that make the individual apathetic, or worse, lead to panic. In this imaginary identification with the powerful, Fromm found the seeds for fantasies of belonging and domination. Among leaders, the fantasies provide the grounds for sadism; among their followers, these fantasies are the seeds of masochism. In this "universal demand for leadership," Read found the sources not only of sado-masochism in social life but an apt description of the corrupt relationship between the Fuhrer and his people in Nazism (1963:55). It would be a tragedy if appeals to heroic individualism should lead to the emergence of egoistic leaders in whose freedom the mass of individuals would fancy themselves to be free, and in whose person they would imagine themselves to be united. We are all too familiar with the dangers of *Super*-individualism that arise from the ritualization of conflict.

Anarchist thought, I suggest, notes that the obstacles to free and assertive individuals lie in the same motives as the danger posed by heroic action. The danger is that leadership will appeal to the "infantile longing to be led": the desire to recreate at the level of the nation-state the very ties and the same tensions that unite individuals in families (Read 1963:56). That is why Read—with other anarchists—insists that the state as an institution must go. In the shadow of the state, all forms of leadership take on the same grey hues; all leaders, except the most heroic and pacific of rebels, become mere politicians seeking and promising the power offered by the state itself. So long as there is a state, its power will be the prize, and its presence will be debilitating to all competitive forms of authority. Read argues that the state, by the sheer weight and scope of its presence, destroys the spirit of a people; it cripples the imagination of the worker and saps the joy of a civilization (1963:78). This is an apt description of the stultifying effects of the cult of authority. In a secular society, that cult is dead. For a society to become wholly secular, therefore, individuals will need to acquire the courage to attack the state without falling under the spell of a new leader. In the next sections of this chapter, I review some of the psychoanalytic literature in order to focus on the internal barriers to the development of such courage.

Barriers to the Spirit of Revolt: Psychoanalytic Understanding of Fear and Helplessness

Before the time at which Read was musing about the obstacles to heroic individualism, psychoanalysts had been observing in detail the tendencies of their patients to avoid conflict and anxiety by imagining themselves to be united in some way with the person who is the object of their desires, and recent studies make these tendencies even clearer. The wish for a symbiotic relationship, or for fusion, serves a variety of psychological needs, not all of them defensive. Some patients think of themselves as "being one with the good mother" and so protect themselves from directly feeling either aggressive toward their mothers or guilty of incestuous strivings toward them; other patients may simply feel more secure and therefore willing to face their internal conflicts (Silverman, Lachmann, Milich 1982:215). A person who feels at one with someone he or she loves may therefore feel less rage at being excluded from a relationship, although fantasies of oneness with another person may also provoke feelings like shame that cause problems of their own (ibid.:209, 216–17). Since individuals who are called up to stand apart from others, to take risks and to assert themselves, will therefore risk feeling frustrated and excluded, anxious and alone. It is not surprising that leaders seek to reassure their followers of their unity with the leader, who will never abandon them to their own devices or let them suffer alone.

The same reassurances, however, are counterproductive in reinforcing the very passivity and fantasies of being loved that stand in the way of effective and responsible, disciplined and risky self-assertion. It is not surprising that the Christian religion not only promises its followers that they must suffer and die for their beliefs, but that their leader will never leave them; neither is it surprising that Christians, consoled by the promise of union with their leader, often neglect to take the heroic actions prescribed for them by the prophets and radicals among them.

The same clinical observations help to explain why fantasies of oneness not only ward off anxiety, perpetuate passivity, and permit some self-examination, but also stimulate grandiose strivings for recognition and authority. When a child identifies with a parent, the child's voice becomes, at least in imagination, at one with the voice of the parent. Through the child speaks the voice of tradition and authority; the child thus learns, through fantasies of fusion with his or her parents, to speak "ex cathedra" (Silverman, Lachmann, Milich 1982:235). Silverman, et al., quote with approval Erik Erikson's (1958:264) dictum that religion gratifies "the simple and fervent wish for a hallucinatory sense of unity with a maternal matrix," and in Luther's case, as Erikson has argued, that hallucination had profound effects on the course of Western culture. To maintain the dream, Luther would have had to exclude the father in order to enjoy the imagined union with his mother— a feat of the imagination expressed in the notion of a highly abstract and transcendent God who, thus elevated, could hardly be encountered in the course of everyday affairs.

The same absence of a fatherly deity also permitted the son to speak *ex cathedra*, a form of speech that ultimately provoked church fathers to retaliate against this newly authoritative voice in their midst. The point, of course, is that the same fantasies of fusion with a parental figure not only foster passivity and helplessness but open the door to grandiose self-images that, acted upon in everyday life, may draw fire from a wide range of local authorities. It is not surprising, therefore, that anarchist thought warns against the hunger for power that, once it dominates leadership in the anarchist movement, may provoke retaliation from the movement's enemies while fostering and prolonging the "infantile" wish of the followers to continue to be led in the right direction. Anarchism therefore warns against the motives that foster both helplessness and premature or grandiose claims to authority. These tendencies toward super-individualism that appear in a fully developed cult of authority, of course, are present from the outset, from childhood onward.

The childhood desire for fusion is at the root of the longing for a common fate, a longing largely unconscious, if not entirely so, and masked under a variety of conscious thoughts and wishes that may appear to be realistic and progressive (cf. M. Klein, 1950). Freud (1962) speaks of the desire for Nirvana, a pleasant equilibrium and fusion with the universe, like the experience of the fetus in the womb. Durkheim (1964) spoke of the "disease of the infinite" in which any limits to human fulfillment are abhorrent and no possession or achievement or relationship is enough. Totalism is another word (cf. Erikson 1969 1970; Lifton 1967) used to signify the attempt of the self to become coterminous with a larger and external whole and so to become at one with some universe, with a family or community, with a nation or with the cosmos. What unites these separate terminologies, moreover, is their common awareness that the desire for fusion invariably has consequences that are destructive either to the self, to others, or to both. In Freudian mythology, Eros unbound leads to Death, the most common fate of all. The rebel, then, must have a clear sense of his or her own boundaries if revolt against the sovereignty of the state is not to turn into one more authoritarian movement. There is nothing in common between the true rebel and the Stalinist-at-heart.

The desire of the self to expand its boundaries and thus to include more of the external world is potentially positive, of course; it is the desire of the organism to incorporate the outside world for additional nourishment and protection: a desire for survival through incorporation. That desire may fuel curiosity and even sympathy as the self seeks to incorporate the experiences of others; the same desire may lead to useful exchanges and corporate mergers. Underneath these positive and progressive forms, however, lies the grandiose wish that implicitly knows no bounds and resents all boundaries. The desire for fusion, for instance, may lead an individual to know others intimately and to be known fully in return; the same desire, left to its own devices, however, may lead the individual to demand perfect knowledge of others and to violate others' privacy or intimacy or to demand limitless attention and total recognition. What varies from one person to the next, then, is not only whether the desire is more or less intense or conscious, but whether the desire is more or less realistic or adaptive in respecting the limits of others. Rebellion without such regard for the "other" has the potential to become demonic.

The desire for fusion, when mixed with a desire to dominate or eliminate rivals does indeed demand ceaseless tribute and become demonic. When individuals, in fact, have the capacity to control others, they are capable, at the very least, of making themselves the focus of constant and favorable attention. Some societies bestow the capacity for controlling the response of others on relatively few, on priests and Brahmins, lords and ladies, on knights and nobles, and even on one personage above all others.

Other societies open the competition for attention to a wide range of actors; social life then becomes an arena in which large categories of individuals compete for others' understanding, affection, and respect. As such competition becomes more universal, the desire for fusion becomes harder to satisfy. Some individuals may therefore turn to symbolic projects that place them outside the competition; e.g., absorption through mysticism into a realm of external objects may become an increasingly attractive project to many seeking distraction from the pain of being unable to imagine themselves at one with others in their social universe. There is no more common a fate, in the end, than such mystical union. It is entirely compatible with, and may reinforce, the "political religion" of sovereignty.

Precisely because it is unrealistic, however, the desire to merge with other selves not only inspires dreams of glory but perpetuates a feeling of helplessness. The combination of helplessness with an unrealistic sense of being known and understood by others in the community may at times be dangerous. I have already mentioned (in Chapter 1) the mining community in West Virginia, described by Kai Erikson in which the miners cherished the illusion of being one with the surrounding hills, of being understood and loved by members of their own community, wrapped up with familiar possessions, sights, and sounds. In adulthood, these miners and their families were therefore tragically incapable of realistically assessing the dangers posed by a makeshift dam at the head of the valley, behind which waste waters from the mines were gradually reaching a devastating volume.

Certainly, the illusion of being in benign surroundings led the community to believe that it was protected by the mining company. Erikson makes it clear that the company's paternalism was matched by the community's desire to be protected and cared for like children in the family. When the dam broke, the community was literally washed away by the waters that had been accumulating for years. Betrayed by their natural surroundings, abandoned by a company that behaved like an adversary after the disaster rather than as a parent, the survivors turned to one another for support, but could not find it. Each survivor was bereft of what had become indispensable aspects of their identities: possessions washed away, keepsakes from older generations buried in the mud, personal landmarks torn from them. In the absence of these signs of their former selves, few members of the community were strong enough to support one another. Their depression was profound, longlasting, and may have nourished a desire on the part of many for the fate of those who died in the flood. The world became disenchanted, and even their religious beliefs seemed irrelevant or useless. None of their obligations seemed to be vital or longlasting; some felt they had only themselves. The flood swept away a sacred universe and caused an abrupt, drastic, and crippling form of secularization, in which death anxiety was conscious, chronic, and, when it rained, often acute.

In summary, the desire for fusion is a desire to turn back the clock to a period in the individual's life that was at once more threatening and apparently more secure. As a very young infant, the child fails to distinguish between the inner and the outer world (O'Keefe, 1982:269, 274–75). The mother disappears, and the child feels that all is lost. When the mother walks out of the room, the child feels as if he or she is dying. If the parents appear distressed, the child feels, with an alarmingly sympathetic magic-of-the-mind, as if those external feelings were internal, so vague is the boundary between the inner and the outer world. Because the child's distress is so intense, the child seeks control through the illusion that what goes on internally can produce results in the outside world. Through a magical reversal, the child speaks and the mother reappears. Here lie the origins of certain kinds of prayer and of the desire to speak *ex cathedria;* in either event one's word has immediate results.

Magical thinking in the infant, then, seems realistic because the child fails to make distinctions between mental operations and external happenings. The child desires to be complete, to restore a lost unity between the one part of the self that is hungry and what seems to be the other part of the self, a part that is not for the moment available. Once the external object is back in the child's presence or mouth, the child feels complete again, and once again fully alive. To push something away and take it back again, like the mother's presence or breast, is a way of magically doing and undoing the self, of making the self whole and of risking the self, if only for the pleasure of making the self whole once again. Infantile magical thinking rejoices in doing and undoing, separating one part of the self from another and bringing back again what was momentarily lost. In this way the child learns to feel in control, to overcome the anguish of feeling helpless, and to feel able to guarantee a fresh victory over psychic death (O'Keefe 1982:269). In this process, therefore, we observe the psychic roots of the desire to ritualize conflict by going through certain motions that are intended to prevent a terrible disturbance from occurring.

Infants may believe that they can eat something, like the mythic apple in the Garden of Eden, that will guarantee them a victory over death; the child is, in his or her thinking at least, godlike. If the child feels that the future knows no terror and holds no surprises, that the outside world is wholly comprehensible and within its grasp, the child has the knowledge of good and evil and is therefore like God. Psychoanalytic literature has for some time compared the Eden myth with the child's earliest wish never to suffer the anxiety and anguish of being incomplete, alone, and unable to guarantee its own spiritual existence (O'Keefe 1982:272–73). The choice faced by the infant is between Hubris and illusory grandeur on the one hand, and, on the other, panic and despair. Here, finally, we observe the psychic origins of the capacity of superindividualism.

The Desire for a Common Fate: Grandiosity, Despair, and Remorse vs. True Secularity

As Niebuhr himself puts it, in speaking of the Reformation's attack on magical answers:

> The Reformation understands that . . . all answers transcend the categories of human reason. Yet without these answers human life is threatened with skepticism and nihilism on the one hand; and with fanaticism and pride on the other. For either it is overwhelmed by the relativity and partiality of all human perspectives and comes to the conclusion that there is no truth, since no man can expound the truth without corrupting it; or it pretends to have absolute truth despite the finite nature of human perspectives (1953:149).

Religion, then, is one place where the battle is waged between the infant's grandiose imaginings of magical control of the world and the infant's anxiety that the world will fail to offer even the possibility of wholeness and salvation. The battle waged in the soul of the child is fought out with the counters of the intellect, on religious battlefields and in the academies, between ecclesiastics and between true believers inside the churches and on the streets. What begins as magical thinking in the child ends up as a desire for a universe that is comprehensible and therefore completely susceptible to mental manipulation. The cult of authority begins in the infant's search for thoughts and words that will prevail over the fragmentation of the world and over the death of the soul.

Of course, it is not only religion that offers a field in which the battle is waged between anxiety or despair and imaginary virtues or powers. Pride and anguish are the poles within which all attempts are made to develop a culture, whether the culture is scientific or religious, cultic or political. In opposing the magical beliefs and practices of the Catholic Church, even the Reformation reflected the initially magical notion that new ideas can change the world. As O'Keefe puts it: "The magical principle works because it *is* action, mental 'action' in the Weberian sense, which is already the beginning of 'social action,' mental action directed against the first outposts of social reality which are inside us" (ibid:275). In the Reformation's attack on the papacy and on the paternal authority of the church, reason was indeed at work against superstition, but one can also detect in that Reformation the magical thinking of the child who claims a right to fulfillment over and against the powerful forces of a world allied and organized against its primal wishes: "One little word shall fell them" (M. Luther). The roots of magic are still intact even when the adult takes a stand against oppression by the irrational authorities of church and state, market and academy (cf. Erikson, 1962). On the way toward a secularized society, therefore, there are plenty of opportunities for the spirit of revolt to become inflated and pretentious or else stifled by renewed oppression.

Niebuhr's warning that culture in the West vacillates between despair and overweening pride may seem melodramatic if one forgets the continuing force, even at the most abstract levels of intellectual life, of the wish for a common fate. It is a wish to overcome not only partial intellectual perspectives but the feeling of being, by oneself, only an incomplete part of a whole that is unattainable. Through a common fate one may overcome loneliness, isolation, and anxiety by entering, if only in one's own mind, a symbolic universe centered in one's own thought. As Niebuhr reminds us, the same desire informs the thought of early social scientists who, with Rousseau, had "confidence in the possibility of bringing all competing wills into the concurrence of a general will" (1951:6). Whether, through science and education, the attempt is to free politics from all irrational forces, or to trust the process of evolution to lead to a "universal community," the wish for a common destiny bespeaks the deepest roots of a desire for fusion; the roots are intact, no matter how elaborate and apparently rational are the intellectual or cultural branches (1951:4–5). Even in a secularized society, therefore, the desire for fusion may stimulate renewed desires for a sovereignty which, like death and taxes, falls on everyone and unites them in the bonds of a common fate.

Sin, as Niebuhr 1953, 1:241–264 reminds us, is only partly conscious; it resides in the unconscious wish of the individual for a total unity of which one is the author and center. Sin therefore leads the adult to manifestly proud and pretentious systems of thought, but these systems disguise an underlying despair at an unresponsive and unreliable universe of which one is only an insignificant part. Sin, therefore, is the refusal to face the facts of one's own incompleteness and relative powerlessness in a world of competitors and frustrating authorities. Paradoxically, an awareness of sin can prevent rebellion and revolt from being romantic and grandiose, but the same awareness without faith can stifle the spirit of revolt itself.

To sin, then, is to defend oneself against despair: "This truth, which the self, even in its sin, never wholly obscures, is that the self, as finite and determinate, does not deserve unconditioned devotion" (Niebuhr 1953, 1:206). As a defense against such truth, pride works two ways: "The pretension of pride is thus a weapon against a feared competitor. Sometimes it is intended to save the self from the abyss of self-contempt which always yawns before it" (Niehbuhr, 1953:7.198). The alternative is despair, not only over the impossibility of receiving total responses and nourishment from a world that does not easily yield to magic, but remorse over "the recognition of the lie involved in sin without any recognition of the truth or the grace by which the confusion of dishonesty might be overcome" (Niebuhr 1953, 1:205).

Sin is a coat of many colors, but Niebuhr painted it primarily in two tones; first, the more vivid hue of magical thinking that places the individual in the center of the world of the individual's own imagining; and second, the beige tones of remorse over having conserved the self so deceitfully. The latter sin is remorse over the first sin, which is an offense against the truth. Despair over never being the object of unconditional love breeds a compromise with reality that is itself the source of a secondary despair, of a derivative self-hatred, more chronic than the first acute anguish at not being able to command the love one needs in order to feel real, whole, and alive.

Niebuhr's analysis of sin soon becomes more sociological. Not only is the primary sin of anxiety followed by the secondary sin of self-deception; the locus of deception lies between sinful individuals in a world that conspires to perpetuate a mutual self-delusion.

> If others will only accept what the self cannot quite accept, the self as deceiver is given an ally against the self as deceived. All efforts to impress our fellow men, our vanity, our display of power and goodness, must therefore be regarded as revelations of the fact that sin increases the insecurity of the self by veiling its weakness with veils which may be torn aside. The self is afraid of being discovered in its nakedness behind those veils and of being recognized as the author of the veiling deceptions (Niebuhr, 1953:7.207).

The implicit reference here is clearly to the fig leaves and lies of the Garden of Eden, of little use in defending the nakedness of the selves that had colluded to protect one another from their insufficiency, vulnerability, and manifest (when naked) incompleteness and separation. Sin, in this variation of Niebuhr's analysis, is social, although it has its roots within the psyche at the moment of despair. This social sin reinforces the individual's self-deception and remorse through adult life and perhaps to the very end. Because that sin is social, it is all the more universal, intractable, and beyond individual efforts to recall. Few can expose their own nakedness, for instance, without risking the concealments of others who have adopted the same illusions about themselves. That is why social conflict becomes ritualized and develops protective layers of complexity and abstraction. Each layer protects the parties to the conflict from being fully exposed to their own vulnerability or to the unjustifiable nature of their demands.

Regardless of how many pretensions a nation may enjoy, regardless of how self-righteous or deluded a particular ethnic group or local community may be; these collective representations are the result of personal faithlessness. Granted that individuals are guilty when they knowingly tout the virtues of their race or nation, or consciously refuse to recognize their own or others' more destructive intentions. The underlying and prior fault is the sin of unbelief; underlying because it is covered by the apparent faith of the patriot or racist; prior because it occurs earlier in time than the later pretensions and makes delusions of grandeur or of security the more necessary as defenses against despair. No wonder, then, that Niebuhr must argue that "Sin is both conscious and unconscious" (1953, 1:250). It is as if Niebuhr were issuing this warning to Western nations: Do not think that you are immune to collective self-destruction in the fascist manner. Social conditions may vary enough, and a nation's history may be sufficiently unique to delude you into feeling protected against such a fate. The seeds of that fate, however, are deeply planted in the soil of the human psyche. Plow deeply enough and you will find these seeds, however long dormant, capable of generating a luxurious and fatal growth. Under certain conditions, and so long as the sovereignty of the state persists, secularization is unstable and may revert to fascism.

The unconscious aspect of sin requires a theory of the unconscious that Niebuhr, in his impatience with psychoanalytic thought, does not fully develop. It is not clear from Niebuhr's discussion whether the unconscious experience of an anxiety unredeemed by faith is a residue of the infant's earliest relationship *after* the child has come to recognize the distinction between the self and others, or whether unbelief and anxiety, the "prior" sin, derives from the situation in which children can not yet distinguish their own responses from the feelings and movements of the world. I suspect, however, that the sin of anxiety arrives once the child learns that there is no magical continuity between the child's movements and others' responses; then the child can experience what the adult would recognize as sheer terror. It is the unconscious memory of that terrifying sense of being isolated and helpless that is indeed "prior" and through the unconscious remains "underlying" the adult's later strivings to be at one with at least some sovereign part of the known social world. Sovereignty is indeed, both in theological and psychoanalytic terms, a fact of social life that derives from an original sin.

Nowhere is it foreordained, however, that individuals should continue in adulthood to express their anxiety by fearing the state or to defend themselves from such anxiety by identifying with the state. They may indeed learn to cope with anxiety, even with death-anxiety, in ways that do not make the state the object either of moral obligation or of fatal attraction. It is clear, however, that unbelief and anxiety are likely to increase, since most complex societies are tied together more by rules or temporary political exchanges than by any enduring emotional ties or broad agreement on values. Furthermore, in the routines of education, work, politics, and even of leisure time, individuals may find their relationships increasingly cool; specialized around specific tasks; temporary; and impersonal even where the rules of the relationship call for the individual to reveal personal information. A society of limited, temporary, and specific obligations is not likely to foster any delusions of collective grandeur; neither is community life in a secular society likely to sustain illusions of safety or belonging.

Under these conditions, even intimacy is increasingly pursued according to rules learned informally in the competitive struggle for friendship and love, or more formally, under the guidance of popular experts in winning friends, influencing people, "fighting fair" with an "intimate enemy," or managing responsible exchanges. In an increasingly secular society, magical aspects of thinking find little anchorage in social life beyond the individual's own routines (idiosyncratic practices that may become increasingly obsessive because they must compensate for increasing feelings of isolation and helplessness). If the typical mental illness in such a society is not obsessive, Lasch (1969) may well be right in pointing to the widespread and chronic narcissism that makes individuals profoundly anxious when alone, for fear they will be abandoned. It is not a comfortable society in which to cope with death-anxiety, but such anxiety may be the price of freedom.

In any society, then, the underlying anxieties of childhood may reinforce the anxious concerns of adulthood. Underneath whatever serenity or reasonableness the adult can achieve may lie the more or less unresolved anxieties of adulthood. It is difficult in any age to measure the quality of life in childhood let alone in later years as adults attempt to speak for themselves, and there is still much to be learned about childhood under the conditions of increasing divorce rates and single parent homes. The point, however, is the same: whatever insecurities remain from childhood in any adult will be stimulated again and again by the competition, fragmentation, and uncertainty of social life in a society that resembles an arena rather than a family. In a truly secular society, will the besetting sin be unbelief, and will it necessarily result in despair, or in pretension and remorse? The answer depends largely on the individual's passage from the family to the institutions more directly related to the community itself and the schools. I will touch on some of these in later chapters.

Death-anxiety and the unconscious sin of unbelief may become more difficult to identify, the more orderly a society becomes. Because the struggle against anxiety cannot so easily be carried out externally in a society that defers consideration of the irrational to leisure time and to the private sphere, individuals will be more likely to "*act* normal" rather than to dramatize their internal suffering. In the next chapter, then, I take up the anarchists' criticism of *normalcy.* Here, I wish only to point out that a desire to have one's experience shared and confirmed through others' perceptions and feelings underlies the drive to ritualize social conflict. Rituals indeed require that others pay a price for one's own suffering; they are sublimated forms of sadism. The routine discharge of sadistic impulses thus occurs in such ritualized forms as professional practice, office management, the processing of clients, and the making of administrative or public policy. Of course amiable political leadership masks private sorrow and deflects criticism from public policies that are in effect sadistic in broadening the distribution of misery among more politically vulnerable social strata. Under these conditions, the consequences of individual despair and pretension are both more widespread and more difficult to identify precisely because they occur in the "normal" course of social life.

Of course, in American society, at least, we can observe strong tendencies to ritualize social conflict. Precisely as the nuclear family gives way to smaller units less able to sustain their members, the more will individuals seek politicaly to turn the larger society into a surrogate or pseudofamily. The intense reactions to the keynote address at the 1984 Democratic National Convention signify the public demand for a social system in which one person's struggle stimulates public effort, as a family struggles together to support the efforts of its individual members. As the "magical" aspects of social life are pushed to the periphery by the routine and technical conduct of work and education, public pressure therefore mounts to restore prayer in the public schools and to educate children in "values." A drive may emerge in which the society as a whole seeks to restore the very elements of mutual care and responsibility that have been lost in social life. But these efforts can provide only substitutes and symbols for the relationships and opportunities that have been lost. That is what it means, of course, to ritualize social conflict in the first place.

I am arguing, however, that the cult of authority may no longer reinforce so easily the sovereignty of the nation-state. We live in the aftermath of two world wars, a time which nation-states may well have lost their "magic." Not only do the impersonal routines of bureaucratic states work, as Weber suggested, to *dis*illusion the individual, so do national disaster and defeat. The "shrinking" (as

Diamond put it), of magic to the level of individual obsession may take the form of compulsive concern with exercise, diet, personal growth and self-development, consumption, and heightened states of consciousness in a society that offers no collective form of magical self-renewal. Collusion in self-deception will continue to occur in more limited or transient social contexts such as therapeutic groups or between audiences and celebrities, but these antidotes to despair are essentially private and do not require the services of the nation-state.

Niebuhr points out that "by asserting these contingent and arbitrary factors of an immediate situation the self loses its true self. It increases its insecurity because it gives its immediate necessities a consideration which they do not deserve and which they cannot have without disturbing the harmony of creation" (1953, 1:252). The true self cannot enjoy the wished-for significance and security by such attentive and repeated focus on the immediate social world. The problem is *in part* that no matter how much respect and reassurance one receives from one's intimates, there are limits in social life to the amount of significance and security any individual can attain. In part, however, Niebuhr is right, no such guarantees can prevent despair. In the long run, there is no substitute for the maturity that, in a secular society, may be essential if the individual is to be able to tolerate death-anxiety without delusion.

The nation-state is forcing the issue by becoming more threatening and disastrous. Schell, in *The Fate of the Earth*, is stating the simple truth that the only way to face the real dangers of nuclear war is to experience terror and despair. Of course, social life may disintegrate when individuals become realistic and therefore terrified. I would argue, however, that what terrifies many individuals at the thought of a future in which all die together is not the thought of extinction; what terrifies is the quiet, unacknowledged appeal of such a death. This chapter has examined the assumption that the soul's secret desire is for fusion with the parent who provides life itself; certainly, the soul who at an early age cannot separate that parent from itself is scared to death and feels as if it were dying. A modern society is too large and complex, too abstract and impersonal, to satisfy the desire for fusion, and individuals are left with their own strategies for enhancing themselves or for merging with others. One strategy calls for the self never to be outlived by others, the other for the self to live only so long as others survive in whom the self is submerged. The prospect of a nuclear holocaust would satisfy the narcissist that no one has survived him, and it would assure the symbiotic self that he is not left to struggle alone in a world without others. Since there is some of both the symbiotic and the narcissist in all of us, a future in which all die together in the end would be deeply satisfying to the desire for fusion. The self then would have no external limits; nothing would survive beyond the self to make it feel isolated or helpless. There would be nothing to be done or undone, and there would be no further need for magic. Nuclear war is the deep magic that ends all death-anxiety in the frightened or lonely soul. The spirit of revolt, which tolerates high levels of death-anxiety and challenges the authority of the nation-state, may now be an essential development of character and personality without which nuclear disaster is virtually inevitable.

Rebellion and Participation:
The Ritualization of Social Conflict
in Soviet and American Societies

THE ARGUMENT UP TO THIS POINT has favored direct action rather than the ritualization of conflict. When conflict is ritualized, enmities are displaced to another arena; then the original issue is lost, the conflict symbolized, and the participants to the struggle either take on grandiose or greatly diminished proportions. There is, however, an alternative viewpoint that favors the ritualization of conflict, based on a rich and well-developed anthropological literature. Chapter 5 will treat the subject of ritual in more detail. Here, I wish to consider briefly the way my argument runs counter to the prevailing opinion of sociologists and anthropologists who have studied ritual in far more careful detail.

Ritual, according to their viewpoint, is an institution for the management of conflict where violent emotions can safely be expressed. Rituals are primarily useful to the individual or the community in times of transition. When one ruler dies and as another takes the throne, rituals ease the fears of the people and allow for a contained expression of jealousy and rivalry that might otherwise tear apart the comminity. At times of death, similar fears and disruptive emotions are safely expressed, but yet contained within the format of ritual. During times of transition from one stage of life to another, rituals provide a secure context within which individuals can express remorse and violent emotion without undue risk to others or to themselves. Transferred from relatively simple to complex, modern societies, the same viewpoint reaches the conclusion that social life in a country such as the United States is not ritualized enough. If it were more highly ritualized suggests Lasch (1969), violent emotions and self-interested behavior would not tear the fabric of the community, and authoritative statements would carry sufficient weight to be believed. According to this view, it is not the ritualization of conflict that poses a danger to the harmony of modern societies or to the growth of free and creative individuals; just the opposite is true. If work and the family, or if politics, sports, and entertainment were more highly ritualized, individuals would be able to suspend disbelief and let their imaginations expand within the safe framework of the arena and the theater; there another reality would prevail that transcends self-interest, and firm boundaries between ritual and the everyday world would signal authoritative speech and set clear limits on destructive behavior. Play requires ritual if it is to be truly playful; and authority requires the framework of ritual if it is to be wholly trustworthy. That is a brief synopsis of the prevailing i.e., priestly viewpoint. Beware the absence of sufficient ritualiztion that makes conflict dangerous rather than the efforts to ritualize conflict that I have been considering in this study. The differences between the professional viewpoint and my own are, at least on the surface, quite irreconcilable.

These differences, however, are relatively superficial. The prevailing viewpoint is appropriate to communities where the boundaries between members and outsiders are relatively clear. Under these conditions, as Mary Douglas (1973) has convincingly shown us, rituals do heighten the distinctions between insiders and outsiders and rely heavily on "natural symbols" in the process; the body, after all, does provide a rich set of metaphors for what can be incorporated and for what must be excluded or eliminated from the body politic. Again, where societies have relatively clear hierarchies of authority and control, rituals leave no one in doubt about where they stand or what the community will stand for. Here again, rituals rely heavily on "natural symbols"; the body is especially fruitful as a source of images and metaphors for structure and hierarchy in societies where the head is clearly distingiushed from the members of the body politic. In a far more complex social system, however, the social context lacks such clear boundaries and chains of command. Because the community is relatively unable to set limits on the dramatization of conflict, rituals will increasingly resemble theater and entertainment. The political trials of the 1960s and 1970s in the United States are a case in point, and the mass media have turned the courtroom itself into a major arena for popular theater and entertainment. In a society like the United States where the final word is seldom spoken and

ultimate authorities find themselves reversed by changes in legislation, in the laboratory, or by popular opinion, no ritual can
safely pronounce the last word on any subject for very long.
Revision becomes a way of life, and conflict can only be *partially*
ritualized. That is precisely the problem.

Measured by the yardstick of simpler societies, conflict in a
complex social system such as the United States will never be
adequately ritualized. Under these conditions, therefore, the attempt to ritualize conflict makes claims that cannot be satisfied in
the process of manufacturing social fact. In more tightly framed
and highly structured societies, rituals do manufacture social
facts: a new marriage or a new regime, a crime or declaration of
war, a just retribution or a pardon. The innocent become guilty;
strangers become enemies; lovers become spouses; and enemies
become reconciled. In more highly fluid and loosely constructed
social systems, however, rituals cannot produce such highly defined social facts. Little is resolved, once and for all, by the
ritualization of conflict. The process, indeed, is virtually endless.
Appeals go from one court to another, and in one state, New
York, the highest court is not called "Supreme"; it is the Court of
Appeals. That is a good metaphor for a modern society in which
there are other courts to which to appeal—public opinion, the
silent majority, the verdict of history. The Second World War, with
its agonies, like the Vietnam War, is still being fought in the media
and dramatized on the streets in order to make one more appeal to
the court of public opinion. The conflict of previous generations
becomes repeatedly, nearly continuously, ritualized in a wide
range of dramas long after the guns are finally put away.

When conflict is partially ritualized, participation becomes a
mixture of drudgery, self-delusion, and self-defeating contributions to a system that does not take these sacrifices seriously.
Toward the end of this chapter, I refer to the example of a Soviet
feminist who puts the problem very nicely; she argues that Soviet
women "participate in the theater of the absurd" by going
through the partial rituals of work, family life, and citizenship.
They are partially ritualized activities because one acts *as if* one can
indeed make a difference to the system by participating in the
rituals. They are only *partially* ritualized gestures, however, since
nothing one does, in fact, makes a difference. Nothing changes;
nothing is resolved. To partially ritualize social life makes participation only partly serious; participation indeed becomes something of a sham, well-intended, but not taken seriously by those

who control the proceedings. Indeed, so long as nothing changes and nothing is resolved, their authority is effectively maintained. By keeping people engaged in the process of ritualizing social conflict, in fact, no new claims to authority can be made; the perpetuation of old grievances and the continuous process of appeal, in fact, makes it impossible to bring any conflict to a conclusion and to bring any authority once and for all to trial.

Whereas, the countervailing viewpoint I mentioned at the beginning of this chapter calls for a more thorough ritualization of the social system, I would argue the case in precisely the opposite direction. Of course, the problem is that conflict is partially ritualized. But whereas the professional view would say that conflict is "only" or "insufficiently" ritualized, I am suggesting that what appears to be too little ritualization may well be too much. While the prevailing view may be precisely right in a society where boundaries are more sharply defined and hierarchies more clearly structured, in a complex society this supportive context is no longer able to reinforce and carry out the work of ritual. One cannot say in a modern society that the last word has been spoken; "all is" never "said and done." To go through the motions of participating in some partially ritualized social conflict, e.g., between generations in school, between classes at work, or between individuals and authorities in the party politics, is to engage in a sham process of manufacture from which social facts never emerge complete and finished. Modern societies, to put it another way, engage in the planned obsolescence of social facts, so that no decision is final and no grievance finally resolved. Participation in such a system is drudgery; it is self-defeating; and it does depend on carefully nurtured delusions.

When conflict is partially ritualized, the imagination comes only partially into play. Toward the end of this chapter I conclude, with regard to the case of the Soviet women, that the system works most effectively by restricting the imagination of the citizen. On the one hand, the individual identifies with a system that offers protection of sorts against a frightening world. The same system, however, does not care what the individual has to say and has no use for the individual's playful imagination. The individual's attention is diverted, then, to the details of everyday life, in the context of which the self acquires a spurious and temporary sort of significance. As Niebuhr put it with regard to despair, the self can easily become distracted with the contingencies of everyday life as an escape from the burdens of achieving selfhood, but these distractions are only partial and temporary antidotes against despair.

Partially to ritualize social conflict co-opts the imagination and so leaves the self little room in which to play. Conversely, the activities of participation, which could be serious, are only sham. There is no outlet in constructive activity for the individual's most aggressive and destructive impulses. These will therefore find outlets more destructive, perhaps, to the self than to the society, although random acts of impulsive violence may also emerge. Trashing and defacing become the semiritualized gestures of individuals whose selves are wasted or who literally cannot face the world. Even their violence itself becomes indirect, partial, and ineffective.

Two comparisons may make the differences between these viewpoints clearer and show how they relate to quite different social contexts. In the next section, for instance, I will contrast two descriptions of the American situation by anarchists who have written in the early and the latter parts of this century. The first description comes from Emma Goldmann, and describes a society whose state is dramatically ritualized in displays of military and naval power in peacetime; it is a society with little room for the play of dissenting ideas. The second description comes from Paul Goodman, who goes into considerable detail about the relatively greater leeway afforded radicals in the Columbia student revolt of the late 1960s. The latter development shows how the boundaries between protest and direct action are eroded in mere "demonstrations"; there, even those most imbued with the spirit of revolt have their imaginations partially captured by the state and seek its interference in order to resolve the ambiguities and tensions of dissent. In the former case, there is little doubt, either about the ritualized display of military power, or the relatively limited leeway offered the spirit of revolt. Under these conditions the state captures the imagination or fails; the spirit is free to succumb or to revolt.

In the following section of this chapter, I will offer other comparisons of Soviet radicalism at roughly comparable points in time: Kropotkin's account of prison late in the nineteenth century, and most recently, a Soviet feminist's account of the difficulties attending the spirit of revolt in modern Russia. Whereas the boundaries between dissent and participation are most sharply drawn in Kropotkin's accounts of Czarist repression, the modern state has found ways to give its citizens the appearance of partici-

pation while effectively repressing the spirit of revolt. I am arguing that it is the erosion of the boundaries between play and direct
action through the partial ritualization of social conflict that makes
modern Soviet and American systems so effectively repressive.

The American Case

In her essay on patriotism, Emma Goldmann tells the
story of a young soldier named Private William Buwalda, who had
the courage to shake Ms. Goldmann's hand at a public meeting.
For this act of independent thinking, he was punished by his
military superiors, sentenced to three years in prison, and accused
of "a serious crime equal to treason" (1969:139). The case indicates
a state whose authority was clearly defined and executed without
obscure and ritualized gestures of "participation." Independent
thought certainly required a court-martial. At that time, however,
the military could rely on popular jingoism, civic self-interest, and
the courts to reinforce its authority. The society's boundaries were
also highly defended in every sense of the term, "defense"
including the psychological.

Take Goldmann's description of the character forged by the
existence and appeals of a militaristic state. Children love the state
and its symbols, she argued, because their own grandiose dreams
are excited by marches and guns and naval exercises and squad-
rons of fighters in the air. Writing before the First World War, she
noted the lavish expenditures of cities like Seattle, Tacoma, San
Francisco, and Los Angeles on fireworks, food, theater and other
displays to honor the Pacific Fleet as it sailed down the coast. Of
course, she lamented the expenditure of huge sums of money at a
time when poverty, hunger, and unemployment were afflicting
millions of men, women, and children; but her final criticism had
to do with the effect of this military display on the character of the
people, and especially on the children. "Instead of bread and
shelter, the children of those cities were taken to see the fleet, that
it may remain, as one of the newspapers said, "a lasting memory
for the child" (Goldman, 1969:136).

The memory of the state's power, of course, will affect different
children in different ways. The anxious, the timid, and the helpless may feel more anxious and intimidated by the state or, more
secure under its protection. They will learn helplessness, in either
event. Children with more aggressive temperaments and dreams

of glory may find the memory of a theatrical display of military power suggestive of future achievements, heroic destinies, and final triumph over the weak. The state, in both cases, inhibits the character of self-reliance and mutual helpfulness. Even worse, the state reinforces tendencies to sadism and masochism that provide ample case material for psychoanalytic studies and for theological descriptions of original sin.

The state tends to develop the psychological character that it requires, whether that temperament be sadistic or simply bureaucratic, heroic or simply stoic in the performance of official duties, loyal or merely submissive in accepting the common fate of all those who live within the shadow of its institutions. The problem with human nature, as the anarchist would have it, is not the secret wish to commit parricide, or fratricide, or even filicide. The wish is there, but it is only under the auspices of the state that these secret desires become frightening, tempting, legitimate, and, in times of war, entirely feasible. Take away the institutional support that promises a possible fulfillment of these dreams, and the dominance of these murderous instincts will diminish. The problem is that even a democratic state will foster the type of personal character that *it* requires. Since it requires that individuals engage in ritualized acts of participation, it requires a character willing to *act as if* it is engaged in thoughtful and direct action regardless of the individual's effectiveness.

The longing of the people to be cared for and led, along with their desire to turn the tables of misfortune, calls for ritualization that can express and satisfy these ambivalent motives without verging on realistic action. When the state parades its military might and dramatizes its police, however, the actions are sufficiently realistic that the people will remain "like children whose despair, sorrow, and tears can be turned into joy with a little toy" (Goldman 1969:135). Such a state engages not only in war, but in breaking strikes, intimidating demonstrators, and in enforcing the law with occasional cruelty against those who fall within their authority (Goldmann 1969:133–34). The state not only divides workers of one nation against those of another, but dramatizes such feelings of uniqueness and superiority that they are willing to be killed and to kill in defense of their own imagined superiority. Strong social boundaries and systems of command intimidate rather than pacify a population. The state and the death it inflicts provide dramatic enactments of fantasies of domination and submission that confirm rather than erode the boundary between play or demonstration on the one hand, and warfare and repression on the other. There are no war games—just war and peace.

These quotations from Goldmann might suggest that anarchism is an anachronism. What Marcuse once called "repressive toleration" now greets dissent, not the court-martial. Anarchism therefore is open for discussion. Goodman argues that, "for objective reasons, it is now quite respectable to argue for anarchy, pacifism, or both, whereas even a generation ago such ideas were considered absurd, utopian, or monstrous" (1970:144). Paul Goodman cites the currency of anarchist ideas among the young during the 1960s, but, as we shall see, he was not entirely happy with the young as carriers of the anarchist tradition.

Part of his confidence in the revelance of anarchist ideas was due to the recurrent crises in modern states, crises brought on, he argued, by the complexity and centralization of the states themselves. War on poverty, hotlines, wars on cancer, or on the Vietnamese, or on urban decay, all were draconian solutions seemingly called for by break downs in the systems of transit, communication, production, and welfare in the most complex and centralized modern societies. In this dilemma, socialist societies fare no better than capitalist nations in overcoming the problems created by the existence of a state that drains resources, stifles initiative, and expands its powers in order to solve the problems that the state itself has created. Paul Goodman's summary of the benefits of a centralized state puts it simply:

> It could be said that most of the national states, once they had organized the excessive fragmentation of the later Middle Ages, outlived their usefulness by the seventeenth century. Their subsequent history has been largely their own aggrandizement; they have impeded rather than helped the advancing functions of civilization. Evidently in our times they cannot be allowed to go on (1970:143–44).

To resist taxes and the draft, to decentralize authority, and restore power to local communities and neighborhoods, to turn professionals and scientists into self-regulating guilds rather than into front-office personnel representing the state, are steps, Goodman would argue, in the right direction. Ultimately it is the nation-state that must go. Indeed, the more secular a society becomes, the more likely is the state to fall of its own weight as energies are withdrawn from it and reinvested in more productive and human forms of social life. Although the agenda is benign, and the state tolerates discussion of its demise, there can be no doubt that the agenda calls for the dissolution of the nation-state; it is *lèse-majesté*.

One would think that Goodman would be delighted, then, with those who, in the 1960s, called unequivocally for the overthrow of the state, for repossessing institutions, dismantling bureaucracies, disarming the police, and giving "power to the people," but Goodman's enthusiasm for the younger radicals is very muted indeed. In the preface to his afterthoughts on the 1960s, he refuses to "condone their idiocy," describes them as "conning" their elders by accepting the older generation's support while betraying that generation's purposes, and finds them so grossly intolerant that "Do Your Thing" means do *their* thing (1970:xii).

Here I am arguing that the reasons why Goodman became "sour on the American young" are to be found in the ritualization of conflict and its effect on individual character. Once anarchism is open for subtle discussion, conflict becomes transformed to fit the rituals of a democratic polity. Issues are symbolized in ways that express the interests of one generation alone. The symbols become abstracted into party slogans and ideologies. Leadership develops grandiose ideas of its own importance and followers lose their integrity as members of a "cadre" or, worse yet, a mass.

Finally, that loss of integrity is foreshadowed by the development of a character that does not observe clear boundaries between play, ritual, and direct action. Goodman calls for the destruction of a system, based on and protected by the state, that makes life complicated, frustrating, and—in an era of high-technology—dangerous to vast numbers of citizens. The system roughs up people. As Goodman notes, the police did much of the killing in the 1960s. When the young revolt, however, high schools may be burned, but "not even principals or guidance counselors will be hurt" (1970:164). The state, on the other hand, is destructive at home and abroad by what it does and by what it leaves undone; by what it causes others to do and by what it fails to prevent. Goodman was writing some years before the American public was becoming aware that their government was financing Central American élite's death squads; the same administration was giving aid to insurgents in Nicaragau whose own means mirrored the methods of the regime they were seeking to overthrow, was encouraging the swift execution of prisoners awaiting the death penalty at home, and was enhancing the powers of the police to search and seize where previously a warrant had been required. No doubt Goodman would have been even more certain, had he lived longer, that "the most brutal and destructive acts will continue to come from those in power" (1970:164). The point is not, however, to make the nation-state more benign;

Goodman argued that given the size, complexity, and sheer power of such a state, no central authority can be legitimate, and a system such as ours should receive far more challenge in the future (1970:173-74). *The point is that, to confront such a state, to attack its authority, and literally to take the law into one's own hands requires a character that may still be in very short supply whether among the young or among their elders.*

Consider, for a moment, just what character would find it possible to challenge so imposing an authority as the modern state. Such a person would be free not only from death-anxiety, but also from a desire to share a common fate with all those who live within the state's territory and therefore fall under its authority. In purely psychological terms, for instance, one would need to feel neither hatred nor love for such a state; one would have to be free from the ambivalence of those who attack the state in the name of patriotism. Love of country leads patriots to affirm the very constitution that makes the state legitimate, even while they express their hostility to the regime or administration in power. Such mixed feelings confirm the legitimacy of the system and blunt the force of any attack on centralized authority. The anarchist character would therefore need to have expunged from its soul any secret identification with the state, a difficult task in any society whose children stand at attention on days of national observance, salute the flag, and sing the nation's anthems. Otherwise, to attack the state, in which the power of the nation is concentrated, would seem also to be an attack on a part of the self.

Finally, there is, in addition to death-anxiety, ambivalence, and identification, another source of timidity. The individual who protests, even though he or she be a pacifist, is likely to have as much potential for violence as any other person. To project such violence outwardly, to exaggerate the state's tendency to be potent and dangerous, may intensify the individual's own fears of the state; the state's power is frightening enough without being magnified by fears of one's own destructive impulses. If the state is big and powerful, it is doubly important not to imagine that the state is an even bigger and more powerful leviathan. If one imagines that one is facing Gulliver, it is easier to feel even more Lilliputian than one actually is, or to identify with Gulliver himself. It may be far too much to expect the anarchist character to emerge as typical in any generation, no matter how hopeful one may be concerning the young as harbingers of a "new reformation."

Nonetheless, the anarchist may not be at all unusual. In describing the normal process by which children, in fact, grow up, Winnicott observes that children learn through aggressive action what is worth destroying and what must be protected (1964:233). The process requires direct action, not ritualized conflict. Through play and dreaming, but also through hitting and hurting, children learn to know where their own selves end and the world begins; in this way they know it is safe to hurt certain objects without having to become anxious that they are destroying themselves (ibid.:234).

Through direct action, children learn, if they adequately distinguish their own impulses from the world around them, not to be spooked by their own fantansies of mayhem. Not every child is like the player of Pac Man, who seeks to destroy certain ghosts, only to be haunted by the ghosts as the latter return, reinvigorated and with a vengeance, to hunt down the Pac Man. As the Pac Man illustration suggests, however, the destructiveness of a child's aggressive impulses depends on whether the child learns satisfactorily to play and fantasize, to enjoy letting symbols represent the objects of the child's own love and hatred without becoming substitutes for those objects. It is healthy, as Winnicott points out, for a child to lose a toy rather than to try to eliminate a hated younger sibling, or to attack a teddy bear rather than injure the mother (ibid.:236).

I would agree, so long as the symbols do not become solemnized and identified with the real thing. However, the young on whom Goodman soured began to lose their capacity for play; their fun and games, as he called them, became deadly serious, and that is when the destruction began. In this regard, for instance, Goodman recalls the sit-ins during which students took possession of administrative offices. For some students, this was indeed only a "demonstration" to be taken seriously, of course, but not literally; for other students, however, the sit-ins became literal invasions of others' privacy and an attempt to take possession of others' space. At this point, Goodman notes, both the radicals and the administration lose their sense of what is play, however serious, and what is real. Conflict, I suggest, by this point becomes ritualized and therefore very "serious."

In one incident at Columbia, the students voted to leave an occupied building, but their "leaders," still in the name of a revolt against authority, overruled the students in the most authoritarian fashion; similarly, even without a consensus from the faculty, the administration decided to call the police. What followed the police invasion, according to Goodman, were administrative tactics fully as petty and vindictive as any stunts by disenchanted and rebellious students: "The most horrible fact about alienated youth is that they are the children of their fathers. As individuals, the young can be freakish. When the confrontation begins, there is a family resemblance" (1970:154-55). The resemblance is that of devotees who worship at the shrine of authority.

Both generations, it seems, are beholden to a common authority, the state, despite their obvious conflicts of interest. Both sides act out their fantasies in ways that eventually call for the appearance of the state in the form of police and judges. Such a common fate is invoked, I am suggesting, when one side or the other loses the capacity to distinguish direct from symbolic action and acts out aggression in a context that has already ritualized conflict. It is as if both sides knew that they were not fully in command of their aggressive impulses; no wonder that the demonstration turned serious when the student leaders decided to overrule the majority's desire to abandon the administration's offices. "Push" was coming to "shove" among parties neither of whom could trust themselves to avoid violence. It is precisely to protect themselves from their own violence and its consequences that individual citizens invoke a fate common to all and from one who is no respecter of persons; they call upon the state. Since the desire to prevent a disturbance underlies the move from direct action to ritualized conflict, it is not surprising, then, when the same desire issues in a call for the authorities to intervene.

It is important not to confuse demonstrations with direct action; it is equally important not to misinterpret direct action as a "mere demonstration." As Winnicott (1964:236–37) notes, children learn by themselves, when conditions permit, to take responsibility for their own aggressive and destructive impulses; they begin to insist on participating, and on doing something constructive. Woe betide the parent who condescendingly acknowledges a child who is "helping" in some way, "by pretending to nurse the baby or to make a bed or to use the Hoover or to make pastry" (ibid.:237); you can tell that Winnicott knows what wrath is provoked when a child finds himself or herself not being taken seriously in these playful attempts to participate in the life of the family. Laughed at, the child loses a sense of belonging and feels excluded and frustrated, sometimes extremely so. In the same way, the young radicals' demands for a constructive role to play in the society focussed on the notion of "participatory democracy." As Goodman notes, students advocated the town meeting over social engineering by bureaucrats and experts, federalism rather than centralization, progressive education rather than various forms of official or commercial indoctrination (1970:155). The common denominator underlying the wide variety of approaches was the desire for a constructive role to play in the larger society: a society that too often seemed impervious to the impulses that motivate ordinary humans to act, take part, share, and build together a common world (Goodman 1970:162). Deprived of such a common but still open-ended future, individuals are reduced to violence and a common fate; no wonder that "karma" became such a popular term for the fatalistic experience and outlook of those whose revolution failed.

The larger society lacks clear boundaries between demonstration and ritual; all action is therefore liable to be taken either too seriously or not seriously enough. That is what it means to live in a world that is only partially secularized; the boundaries between the sacred and the profane are not clear to anyone, even to the actors themselves. Without an external framework and a set of guarantees, one cannot be sure that all share the same commitment. Without faith, one needs a guarantee that failure will be borne equally by all, and that the outcome will be recognizable as fulfilling the dream that prompted the initial action. The lack of such a frame is especially distressing to those who lack an internal framework of their own.

Speaking of children who may be frightened by their own destructive impulses and their fears of retaliation, Winnicott notes that some find their homes an adequate framework for working out their anger and hatred without destroying what they most love, while other children are fated to search elsewhere and may eventually find only in prison the context for their safekeeping and others' protection (1964:228–29). It is just such a framework, I am arguing, that is lacking in a complex society, where individuals must improvise and trust one another long before the end is in sight or before the limits to one another's tolerance and endurance are known. It is entirely understandable under these conditions that even radicals seek to ritualize conflict. In so doing, however, they reopen the appeal to a higher authority that can pass sentence, and whose word is final.

It is not surprising, but it is nonetheless tragic, that some revolutions substitute for participatory democracy the strong frame suggested by a "cadre"; Goodman's point is apt.

> As a revolutionary political method, cadre formation means the development of a tightly knit conspiratorial party that will eventually seize the system of institutions and exercise a dictatorship until it can shape the majority to the right doctrine and behavior. Etymologically, "cadre" and "squad" come from (Latin) quadrus, a square, with the sense of fitting people into a framework (1970:157).

Instead of trying to work together, to participate, and to be taken seriously for their efforts to find a place in the larger society, some students demanded a more rigid framework, program, duties, and ideology. Winnicott notes that such a framework, for children who have none of their own, prevents some from being too anxious and others from going mad (1964:228). As Goodman pointed out, most of the young radicals were not so anxious that they needed or would accept such party discipline, and, few were power-hungry enough to pose as leaders of such "cadres"; a few, however, did conspire to lead such a disciplined movement and held views of themselves and their role in society that were clearly delusory (1970:157). *It is clear, then, that for a radical movement to remain democratic, to resist authoritarian leaders, and to remain open to change, requires a character that carries within itself a framework sufficiently strong to endure and flexible enough to take advantage of whatever openings a society or chance itself may provide. The enemy of such a movement, as anarchists have long known, is primarily within the self's own aspirations to power and glory.* In the first chapters, of course, we considered this problem under the headings of anxiety, unbelief, and sin, as well as in connection with tendencies to sadism and masochism.

Since anarchists seek to replace central authority with an authority that is more innovative, specific to the occasion, populist in base, and spontaneous in its development, they cannot afford to indulge in grandiose and magical thinking, which in the child may cause bad dreams, anxiety, guilt, and compulsive forms of play, but which in the adult may feed delusions of grandeur and substitute rhetoric for action. It is just such a tendency that Goodman notes in the Leninist-style leaders who tried to take what was good in the students' movement and make it serve the ends of an "advance-guard." Goodman is almost scathing in his comments about student leaders who tried to use "lively energy and moral fervor for a political revolution that will not be, and ought not to be" (1970:158). Young people who thought they were engaged in neighborhood projects or community action did not think of themselves as needing to be made more radical or politicized; such a need was imputed to them, however, by those who claimed to have the end of the revolution already in sight. Not surprisingly, the end they envisaged called for the visionaries themselves to exercise leadership and, where possible, authority over whose who were moved to actions out of a simple concern and moral impulse. As Niebuhr pointed out, all self-delusion requires that others conspire to maintain it. That is, when conflict is displaced from direct to symbolic action, the solemnity of the proceedings serves to guarantee to the participants in such ritualized conflict a measure of unrealistic dignity and self-importance.

It is clear, then, that for individuals to act assertively yet without inviting premature capitulation to the state requires a strong character. Individuals who can distinguish between their own aggressive impulses and those of others can also dramatize their concerns without intimidating others. When taking direct action, they can assert their own authority without dramatizing that authority in the uniform of the state, and they can leave for others as much leeway as they demand for themselves. Such characters are literally free and yet disciplined. They require no external framework for exerting control on others and on themselves, because they have a framework of their own; call it character. It is a character that firmly distinguishes between the self and the world. Such a character experiences little anxiety because it identifies with no external body or authority and therefore is not frightened, so to speak, of its own shadow. That is the long shadow cast by the projection of oneself into an outside world, where one's identity can be found and which mirrors, in exaggerated form, one's own drives for power. The secular character, freed from the burden of unrealistic and grandiose thinking, can work with others in creative and innovative projects that do not precipitate official intervention and protection before the final struggle for successful revolution.

The Soviet Case

Unlike American youth of the 1960s, who had reached early maturity under the not-so-threatening auspices of a democratic state, Kropotkin lived in a Russia that for centuries had been ruled by official state terror. His comment on the fortress of St.

Peter and St. Paul notes what an impact the prison had had on Russian imaginations, "the terrible fortress where so much of the true strength of Russia had perished during the last two centuries, and the very name of which is uttered in St. Petersburgh in a hushed voice" (1962:231). In the *Memoirs,* although his accounts of his own activities are very modest, his activities seem all the more remarkable because of the impact of official terror on the imagination of all Russians. Even the aristocracy was not exempt, since, as Kropotkin goes on to point out, the Imperial family sacrificed its own children and murdered its own spouses along with those who objected to these human sacrifices. It is remarkable, to put it mildly, that the anarchist mind did not live in more terror of official reprisals, especially when such terror might seem to be fitting punishment for those who, like the anarchists themselves, were calling for the overthrow of the state.

Instead of such understandable timidity, we find in Kropotkin's chronicles various accounts of how he, his brother, their colleagues and associates among students, workers, and peasants simply went on with the business of educating themselves and designing a new older, literally, within the shadow of the state, and in daily, realistic expectation of arrest, imprisonment, torture, and death. This is not the place in which to engage in a psychology of the Russian revolutionary or to make precise comparisons with the youth of the students' movements in the 1960s; such a study is beyond my capacity. What I wish to point out is simply that the state need not become a framework within the mind that sets its own limits and needs no magical support from external authorities to control its own aggressive, destructive, and rebellious impulses.

Winnicott's comments about the transformation of aggressive and destructive impulses into constructive, however, symbolic activities offer some clue to the strength of a Kropotkin even in the loneliest and most fearful prison surroundings. There, through the efforts of his brother and colleagues, he was able to continue to work on the papers he was presenting to the Geological Society regarding the nature and extent of ice formation over the Soviet land mass. Like thousands of other prisoners, who had recorded their mental anguish and their struggles for hope and sanity in southern jails or Nazi death camps, Kropotkin found that he could give himself to others in constructive activity, overt or covert, sanctioned or illicit, symbolic or material, directed toward fellow prisoners or distant associates. The totalitarian regime could afford to give Kropotkin this space in which to preserve his own identity. Like the Nazi prison in which Bonhoeffer was incarcerated before his execution, the framework of the state was strong enough to allow certain prisoners the materials for private reflection. Nonetheless, Kropotkin and Bonhoeffer had to create for themselves an internal framework that provided leeway for the spirit, for playful thought and serious design. It is when such a framework is broken that the self collapses and often, then, also the body. The spirit of revolt requires a self that has its own projects and designs so clearly marked that it cannot be co-opted or seduced into rituals of others' design; such a self will also not flounder or collapse when left alone and secluded, or be terrified by internalized images of the state.

To maintain the self is itself a radical act of courage and spiritual strength; not all are able to do so, as Kropotkin himself notes in his sad references to prisoners who went mad within prison, or died of sickness and despair. I am suggesting, however, that there is a form of character destruction that comes from participating in a social system that is antagonistic to the individual. Under these conditions, where a person must, in order to maintain a self, cooperate consciously or unwittingly with a system of oppression, everything that the individual does to maintain a character and to act within that character deprives the self of what it most needs— leeway to play and to grow. That is precisely the problem with ritualizing conflict in a repressive social system. Take, for one example, another description from within Soviet society written nearly a century after Kropotkin's imprisonment, by a woman rather than by a man, who, unlike Kropotkin, was enjoying the formal freedom to go to work and maintain a home. This is how she writes tellingly of a certain madness that attends survival in everyday life:

> The total certainty that one can change nothing is characteristic of the consciousness of the Soviet people. But the thought that their sufferings are without purpose or meaning is intolerable. Anyone can participate in the theater of the absurd, which is what Soviet life is, and not despair or go mad. And there are people who do go mad, all the while telling themselves things that through their own personal experience and common sense, it would seem absolutely impossible to believe (Sariban, in Mamonova, [ed.], 1984:212).

The only way to stay sane under these conditions is to develop what Read called the "spirit of revolt" against an absurd civilization.

To be absurd is to develop the self in ways that serve others' purposes better than one's own; to participate in such rituals is to own burdens and to inhibit, perhaps permanently, the emergence of what might be called one's essential life. Hear again Ms. Sariban as she speaks of the character developed by the Russian women who go to work, return to the chores of housekeeping and shopping, and yet find no exit from this stultifying routine; on the contrary, to carry out their burdensome duties becomes a way of life along which they travel at the risk of their own free development as persons in a free society. The complexity of life becomes a burden that makes freedom seem impossible and even unthinkable; on the other hand, the routines of everyday become as absorbing to them as do the routines of life to a prisoner in a fortress:

> The average Soviet woman's consciousness, and even to a significant degree her unconscious, are rigidly confined to the everyday world. There are several reasons for this. The first is that the practical life of Soviet women, and for that matter of all Soviet people, is limited to everyday concerns much more than is that of people in democratic countries. For nothing in society depends on the individual. No one and no thing takes him or her into account. People do not even have any illusions that their opinions count for something or that anyone is listening to them. The only sphere of activity within their own world and the world around them in which people have some degree of influence (and even this is very limited) is the sphere of the day-to-day. Here they can make some choices and decisions. They can decide what to get, what to buy, what to do (Sariban, ibid.:209).

There is the absurdity precisely stated. To be a self one must have decisions and choices to make, but in that complex society one's choices do not add to one's freedom or increase one's influence; on the contrary, every choice simply compounds the burden of everyday life, further buries one in a mound of detail that, although necessary for survival, is trivial in itself, and makes one so preoccupied that one has no time, thought, or energy left for creating a different system. Women thus discover that in order to maintain their character they must carry a larger load than men and maintain a system that, subjugating them both, burdens them unequally. It would be difficult to find a more poignant or pointed statement of the absurd than this, but that is precisely the cost of partially ritualizing social conflict. Participation imposes burdens and requires sacrifice without manufacturing a new social fact. On the contrary, participating in social life bears all the marks of an obsessive ritual: a *folie à deux* raised to the *n*th power.

The Soviet feminist offers nearly a prototypical anarchist diagnosis of the difficulties of the Soviet citizen. Ms. Sariban notes how difficult it is to get most Soviet women to overcome "traces of an unconditional faith in the fairness of certain assertions made by Soviet propaganda"; a need to be involved with others in meaningful pursuits makes Soviet women susceptible to propaganda and "binds them inseparably with dedication to the Soviet system in its present form and the moral necessity of supporting that system in the face of outside danger and of working selflessly for Soviet power" (Sariban, ibid.:211). Think of what has been packed into the brief psychological analysis of the Soviet woman: several elements, indeed, of problems encountered by women in the United States who are unable to consummate their own rebellion without provoking or inviting repression by the authorities. It is no wonder that Soviet citizens become anxious at attacks on a system with which they identify; indeed, they appear to love or at least respect the same system that they have every reason to hate. As for fears of their own aggressiveness, it may well be that these are projected to the outside world, where Soviet propaganda locates constant and increasing threats to the security of the nation itself. Frightened by propaganda into a premature submission, it is not surprising that they are made doubly anxious by appeals to be more assertive. The self, grandiose because identified with the system, has reason to fear that its own aggressions might have a devastating impact. The self, frightened by its own grand self-image, loses the spirit of revolt.

In many ways, there appears to be a paucity of ideas, ideals, even fantasies of freedom among these citizens and no spirit with which to revolt against an absurd civilization. Sariban reports that "not only is there nothing ideal in the lives of Soviet women, there is not even much simple beauty. Everything is earthbound, banal, and gray" (ibid.: 211). Where is the dreaming, the play with symbols, that serves the child as a prelude to assertion and may serve the adult as a model for transforming the world? The problem here is not only that symbols serve as a substitute for action, in the same sense that symbols distract all those engaged in highly ritualized forms of conflict. There also appears to be little magical thinking among these Soviet feminists, few of whom were led to feel that their rhetoric had actually accomplished something. As for the average Soviet citizen, Sariban finds a paucity even of free speech. When she asks Soviet women about their ideals and purposes in life, she finds their answers "almost always quite incoherent" and "full of contradictions" (ibid.: 210–211). This is a description of a tragic inhibition of consciousness, speech, and imagination. Underneath its grandiosity, the self is really a small and helpless thing whose opinions do not matter and whose actions make little difference.

The spirit of revolt is difficult to find under normal social conditions and exceedingly difficult for those who have experienced oppression. Frantz Fanon (1963), in describing colonial blacks, speaks of a man who, in his dreams, was terrified of soldiers who were pursuing him with their long rifles. Rejecting Freudian interpretations of the guns as phallic, Fanon puts it simply; the soldiers are realistic, oppressive, threatening reminders of the power of the state to subjugate those who rebel. In his dreams, the man was frightened by the possible repercussions of his own aggressive wishes against the power of the authorities. The state, in other words, exists as a real threat in the external world, but the state is also operating within the sanctuaries of the mind, where even in the night it takes its human toll and demands sacrifices of those who have the heart to wish they were free.

It is difficult to overestimate the degree to which the power of the state operates unconsciously to intimidate even the courageous. Consider the mind of one woman, a Chicana whose experiences are recounted in the volume compiled by the Coleses (1978) on women in America (cf. Part three, pp.127ff.). In the story of the Chicana, the Coleses present a woman who had profoundly mixed feelings toward a Mexican-American man who had both punished and yet sought her; he had offered her opportunities that offended her and tried to intimidate her when she refused. He was however, a man toward whom she felt some attraction that she could not easily identify. In one of her dreams, the Chicana finds herself in a street scene, surrounded by men with guns and helicopters. The scene is not unrealistic and may have been partly a reminiscence of a strike of Mexican-American workers, male and female, against a local hotel where she was employed. (In that strike, men and women had temporarily acted in solidarity, although their resistance crumbled under the force of scabs, strikebreakers, and the police themselves.) In her dreams, however, the Chicana finds that *all* the victims are women; even her mother is there, identifiable through her apron. Tied in bonds of suffering to women, in everyday life as well as in her imagination, the Chicana finds that *all* the oppressors are men. Indeed the man who had paid her the attention mentioned earlier, toward whom she had such powerful and mixed feelings, was also there. His name, as it appears in her recollection of the dream, is Peter Diaz; she recalls:

> She had trouble falling asleep that night. And when she did, she dreamed and dreamed. She said, days later, that she had never dreamed so much during a night. Nor could she easily, even months later, shake off the memory of those dreams: "I've always had a lot of dreams, but most of them I forget by the end of the next day. Usually I remember part of the dream when I wake up, but once you're doing things you forget your dreams. But that night I didn't really sleep—I just dreamed and dreamed. The part that I'll never forget was the firing squad. I was in my house, near the door, talking with my mother. Suddenly we heard a noise outside, as if someone was shooting. We opened the door, and we saw police cars, lots of them. The whole street was full of those cars, with the red lights on top going around and around. Then I saw a helicopter, and it landed, like on television, near the police, and some men got out—maybe detectives. I saw the police knocking on one door, then the next. They pulled out people from each house, and took them to a spot in the middle of the street. Some police stood nearby holding their guns, ready to shoot. Other policemen were holding up some rope, a circle of rope. The police took the people to the rope and made them bend under it and stand there, inside . . .
>
> We got to the place where the people were standing. They told us to go under the rope and be still. My mother went, and so did I. The police were staring at us; they had guns pointing right in our faces. I guess I decided to die. I wasn't going to stand there and be sent to jail. I didn't do anything wrong. I left the other people. I went under the rope and started to run away. One of the police ran after me. He told me I was going to be shot. He grabbed me and put me in a car— the Cadillac of Peter's! The driver turned out to be Peter! I asked him where he was taking me, and he said to his dance hall. I said I wanted to get out, but he said I couldn't. He laughed; he said his hand was on the buttons, and they kept the car doors locked.
>
> When he stopped, it wasn't the dance hall we'd come to. We were back where we started! All the people were there in a circle, with the police guarding them. Peter told me I had a chance to escape. I could stay with him. He'd hide me in the trunk of his Cadillac and drive away, and I could live in his office; otherwise, I'd had to get out of the car and be pushed into the crowd. I looked for my

From *Woman of Crisis: Lives of Struggle and Hope,* by Robert Coles and Jane Hallowell Coles. Copyright © 1978 by Robert Coles & Jane Hallowell Coles. Reprinted by permission of Delacorte Press/Seymour Lawrence.

mother, but there were so many people, I couldn't find her. I think I heard her voice calling my name: Teresa. Peter asked me what my choice was. I said to stay—not go with him. He said all right, I would die, and he didn't care. I left the car, and he drove away. Just as I crawled under the rope, the police started shooting. I saw people falling. I was still looking for my mother when I saw someone lying on the ground near me. It was her. She had on her favorite apron. I realized she was dead. Everyone was pushing to get away, but no one could. There were too many police, and they were using pistols and rifles and machine guns.

Then they opened up fire on us from above—the helicopter. I was sure we were all going to be killed, wiped out. I thought to myself that I was too young—that I shouldn't die. But I guess I did. I saw a policeman shooting, and he aimed his gun right at me, and just then I woke up. I think it was Peter who was shooting me—wearing a policeman's uniform! I think we were all women; I think I noticed that before I woke up, or maybe I discovered that when I woke up! Maybe I was looking to see if my father or any of my brothers were there; maybe that was how I noticed that there weren't any men at all there.

Here, then, is a composite figure of men as objects of attraction, as sources of power and authority, as objects of fear and hatred: a composite that includes a father, a possible employer, and the state. The mind fails to discriminate among these symbols of repression; they are the same person, a patriarchal and violent figure whose actions bind women in a collective experience of suffering. This symbolic, collective person becomes a figure of authority, not wholly repressive and unattractive, that binds the spirit of revolt and heightens death-anxiety to the level of panic.

The state, as Read noted, is a reactionary institution because it prevents new forms of social life from emerging. It is reactionary in another sense, the psychological, because once internalized, it acts as a defense against the individual's own aggressive impulses. To suffer the punishment of such a nightmare as the one just described, the individual would perhaps have had to commit, if only in her imagination or even her unconscious, the crime of lèse-majesté or of parricide itself. That was capital punishment being meted out by the men and state in her nightmare; her psychological offense, I am suggesting, was no doubt a capital one. Indeed, the Chicana had had moments in which she imagined that Peter Diaz was dead, and she had enjoyed daydreams in which women turn the tables on men. In one such fantasy she found her husband waiting on her mother-in-law at a hotel table, and she herself came up with the cash for the bill, a fine reversal of fortunes in everyday life. This wished-for reversal, I am suggesting, often incites the imagination to react in a way that provides a fitting punishment; indeed, in the fantasy of having a man, her husband, serve her mother-in-law, she herself pays for the pleasure of that reversal by paying the bill. The imagination exacts payment even for dreams in which women find themselves turning the tables on men who monopolize opportunity, power, and authority. In the same way, the unconscious law of an-eye-for-an-eye becomes a habitual reaction against the individual's own desires for triumphant satisfaction; internalized in the form of the police, the state becomes a psychological source of repression enforcing that law against the offending imagination. The state, then, as an internal framework must be broken before individuals can freely assert their rights without intimidating others or without fearing reactionary and repressive retaliation by the authorities.

The will-to-live, then, is a strong impulse but it is easily suppressed, distorted, and deflected onto objects that do not sustain life and, in the long run, sap the will to live. There is ample clinical and epidemiological evidence that the isolated, the lonely, and the rejected sicken and die more easily than those who are part of a vital and caring community. There is also ample evidence that those who are too deeply immersed in the community become so absorbed by their relationships that social life becomes heavy, burdensome, and repressive; the will-to-live can suffer then from inertia, custom, tradition, and from the force of the state's own particular authority. Indeed, as Stirner put it, the state becomes a part of the mind itself, a complex as independent and obsessive as any neurosis:

> The State is the lord of my spirit, who demands faith and prescribes to me articles of faith, the creed of legality; it exerts moral influence, dominates my spirit, drives away my ego to put itself in its place as "my true ego"—in short, the State is sacred, and as against me, the individual man, it is the true man, the spirit, the ghost. (1845, 1971:213).

It would be hard to find a more exact description of how the self, inflated by its identification with authority, deflates itself. The cult of authority destroys its own devotees.

The state, furthermore, dissolves and destroys those communities in which the individual learns reciprocity and freedom through mutual aid; in the place of services individuals and groups render to one another, it provides its own services. Certainly the history of the "welfare state" is a chronicle of all those forms of aid once rendered through voluntary organizations, private hospitals and other institutions, through political parties once rooted in ethnic communities, able to provide help and jobs through the "patronage system." In their place are various forms of insurance, the abstract wage and industrial policies of the state, and a vacuum left by the disappearance of the more local and community-based forms of mutual aid. In this process, the will-to-live becomes increasingly directed toward goods and services provided by the state. The drive toward freedom becomes easily suppressed by the force of public opinion, by state-sponsored education, and by threats of reprisal by the state and its agencies. The force of an abstract majority "opinion" and often of the law itself can always be used to suppress a vitality that does not serve the purposes of the state.

In focussing on the state, of course, I have been selecting only one, admittedly forceful and pervasive authority, whose presence through the letter of the law kills the spirit of unsanctioned mutual aid, of individual conviction, and of rebellion itself. The state, of course, can reinforce the repressive tendencies of custom and public opinion, can support the domination of small communities by large bureaucracies and large corporations, and can further elaborate the regulations affecting work and a wide range of social life to the point of such complexity that no individual can comprehend more than a fraction of his or her opportunities and potential liabilities. In the next chapters, while I will still focus on the state, I will attend also to the repressive effects of complexity, of large-scale organization, and of habitual and institutionalized patterns of social life.

What concerns the anarchist in this case is not merely the actual repression of the individual by an external force, such as the state, but the effect of ritualizing conflict in the daily life and ordinary transactions of the society. The ties that bind people together and limit their freedom depend on implicit understandings; these taken-for-granted, virtually unconscious assumptions deprive people of the opportunity to act spontaneously and to act together to satisfy their common needs.

> Far be it from us not to recognize the importance of the second factor, moral teaching—especially that which is unconsciously transmitted in society and results from the whole of the ideas and comments emitted by each of us on facts and events of everyday life (Kropotkin 1927; 1970: 138).

Here Kropotkin is looking for what Freud called the "inhibitions": those internal monitors that examine the individual's profoundest wishes, accepting some, rejecting others, but on the whole disguising them so that they are incapable of becoming fully conscious and therefore of achieving direct satisfaction. Moral teaching, in other words, is the form that repression takes in a society whose ultimate form of repression is the state itself; in that society, however, the state relies on a set of governors who appear in the familiar forms of teachers, parents, friends, and guardians—sources of moral teaching. Freud was quite explicit about this analogy between the mind and the State; indeed, he sounds something like an anarchist himself:

> Our mind, that precious instrument by whose means we maintain ourselves alive, is no peacefully self-contained unit. It is rather to be compared to a modern State in which a mob, eager for enjoyment and destruction, has to be held down forcibly by a prudent superior class (1963:303).

That class is so prudent, in fact, that the State relies far more on teachers and parents, clergy and social workers than on the police and the troops, whose work only really begins when the sources of instruction and of moral teaching have failed. Indeed, it is far easier, as Bakunin reminded us, to revolt against the State than it is to overthrow the authorities that speak to us from all the familiar faces and places: X

> The action of social tyranny is gentler, more insidious, more imperceptible, but not less powerful and pervasive than is the authority of the State. It dominates men by customs, by mores, by the mass of prejudices, by the habits of daily life, all of which combine to form what is called public opinion.

> It overwhelms the individual from birth. It permeates every facet of life, so that each individual is, often unknowingly, in a sort of conspiracy against himself (1972:239).

Just as it is the individual's conspiracy against himself that permits his contradictory wishes and fears to be painfully held together in a neurosis, the same conspiracy of people against themselves provides the focus for the anarchist's analysis of social contradictions. On the one hand, Kropotkin speaks of "tendencies": the last flickering of the will to revolt; or the easily repressed but eventually irrepressible desire of the will of each person to unite freely with others in common action, in Freudian terminology, the principles of eros and of the ego (1963:125ff.). On the other hand,

Kropotkin notes the presence in society of "institutions," habitual ways of thinking and acting, that perpetuate the unequal and aloof relationships between governors and the governed, the wealthy and the poor, men and women, and individuals of different places and nationalities. Through an "analysis of society," Kropotkin writes, one can encourage a society's characteristic tendencies and "work for the destruction of the institutions" (1927, 1970:141). Freud could hardly have put it better, although he might have spoken of dismantling the character structure of an individual in order to provide free play for those instincts for survival and loving relationships that had been contained under the crust of habit and hidden behind the armor of an individual's defenses.

Coda

For centuries, elites have used complex rules and regulations to dominate groups of lower status. Kropotkin (1970:251–52) makes this point in some very telling illustrations; e.g., in the Third Republic, the signatures of various bureaucrats in "the ministries of interior and finance" were required on more than fifty documents to effect the removal of a tree that had blown on to a national highway. Basil Bernstein argues that the middle and upper classes have developed a more elaborate form of speech, one that requires learning in childhood if one is to master it. The effect is to perpetuate the domination of higher over lower classes who understandably find such speech awkward or inaccessible. Such complexity, however, is hardly the monopoly of modern societies. We still use the word "Byzantine" to recall the elaborate intrigues and deceptions by which an empire by that name mystified and dominated an entire population. We need no reminder that the original labyrinth was made by Daedalus, according to the myth, at the behest of the King of Minos, as a symbol and an instrument of that king's rule. "Sanskritization" has become a term for the way any elite places its own form of communication beyond the reach of all outsiders. The word reminds us that to ritualize social conflict creates a class of "Brahmins" who own and control the rituals of social interaction.

Domination through complexity is the function of all forms of code—legal, linguistic, mystical; but it is a technique, however, that can be self-destructive. Regimes may become so tangled in their own complex rules and bureaucratic organization that they are unable to respond quickly and flexibly to new situations. Even rebels, furthermore, know how to make use of complex designs to thwart those in power. In this chapter, then, I argue that groups use complexity in language and in social organization to perpetuate their domination, but that in so doing, they mortgage their effectiveness to the forms by which they claim to be legitimate rulers. The cost of ritualizing conflict is to make even those in power obligated to preserve the forms of address and of adjudication by which they exercise their authority.

The more conflict is ritualized, the more likely it is that collective functioning will take precedence over the needs and wishes of specific individuals. Of course, smooth collective action is not always repressive, even if it is ritualized. Kropotkin (1970:215) believed that all members of primitive tribes engaged in hunting and food gathering, and that private property was not inherited; he wanted to assert that local custom, however ritualized, need not perpetuate domination. Bakunin, however, is more adamant in rejecting mores and customs as a form of "social tyranny" (1972:239, 241). In this chapter, however, I am arguing that, as social conflict becomes ritualized, the complexity of the rituals of social interaction, combined with the complexity of the system itself, makes people into what (following Dobbelaere and Luhmann) I have been calling "dupes" of the social system.

The anarchist project, i.e., the emancipation of humankind from all forms of order except those arrived at by continuous and spontaneous acts of free consent, requires that the state be replaced with more flexible, simpler, and smaller forms of collective organization. For Kropotkin, the state was the evil "principle that destroys everything" (1970:252). He was thinking of the way the state inhibits or destroys all forms of organization and control except those sponsored by the state itself; the peasants, for instance, are discouraged from organizing their own communes but are allowed, under the auspices of the state, the right to organize agricultural unions—a Pyrrhic "victory for democracy" (ibid.:252). There is simply no doubt in the anarchist mind that individuals should be allowed to do for one another what they can. To institutionalize health or education, for instance, is to make the process of getting well or learning something a matter for professional guidance and control; to institutionalize learning, then, is to habituate individuals to being guided and justifies the prevailing level of complexity. The argument of modern writers like Jonathan

Kozol or Ivan Illich has insisted on this point. Once individuals become used to going to schools for education or to doctors for getting well, they have already lost the battle for freedom. Medicine has become too complex for the laity, and so has education; conversely, the laity have become accustomed to a way of life that makes them students or patients in an increasingly wide array of activities in which individuals were once left to themselves. Now, as the doctor and the teacher, the social worker and the various other professionals combine to make their authority coercive and their services necessary for the citizen, they receive the protection of the state. As Kropotkin would have put it, where the priest, judge, soldier, and lord combine, there is the state, and the resulting concentration of power destroys all competitors within its territory. For Bakunin, the devil in history was not confined to the formal organization of the state itself; it was the principle of command, a devil that can influence even socialist organizations when they succumb to the authoritarian tempter.

In rejecting the state, then, anarchists have refused to take into their own hands the powers that command consent and discourage competing forms of united action; therein lay the disagreement, of course, between Bakunin and Marx. The same disagreement caused Max Weber to argue that the anarchists' project is anachronistic in view of the size, complexity, and technological advancement of modern societies, for which the state is the only conceivable form of political order. Here, however, I wish to revive the anarchists' argument against the state. The state only appears to be "necessary," I suggest, so long as work, education, health, and other essential activities become sufficiently complex that more communal or spontaneous forms of organization will not suffice, *and* so long as individuals become habituated to being doctored or schooled or otherwise subordinated to professional frameworks. In the absence of adequate rituals for managing social conflict, a highly complex social system lacks the support of custom and appears arbitrary and unmanageable. To the extent that any complexity is supported by ritualized gestures and attitudes of consent, however, an elite's domination will *seem* to provide simplicity, unity, and legitimate rule.

Still, it is not a *gross* oversimplification to argue that complexity in social life is imposed by elites to perpetuate their domination. Complexity is a characteristic of a code, and elites alone control the code embedded in the organization of a social system. The more complicated industry becomes, the more difficult it will be for workers to control it. The more complicated becomes the machinery of state, the more it will be impossible for citizens and workers to take control of it. Whatever complexity is introduced in modern industry becomes a code so difficult to decipher that workers find it difficult to know and understand one another, to share their knowledge and perceive their common interests. Once relegated by the state, however, that complex division of labor becomes a labyrinth into which many enter but from which few emerge:

> Such was the role of the state in the industrial field. All it was capable of doing was to tighten the screw for the worker, depopulate the countryside, spread misery in the towns, reduce millions of human beings to a state of starvation, and impose industrial serfdom. . . . Workers have become separated from their old guilds, whose remains are now . . . battered and overtaxed, these useless cogs in the administrative machine. (Kropotkin 1970:255–56).

The state has become like a large-scale factory. Within it one worker does not know what the others are doing or why they are doing it. Those who live under the shelter of the state, like those who used to live in the vicinity of the factory, have been uprooted from their natural communities and have no other work to do than what is provided for them through the state. Natural forms of collaboration fail to achieve results, but must await the signature or licensing of the state. Life-threatening problems or simply protracted and unnecessary suffering fail to produce collective action, since the rules for taking action are made elsewhere, seldom enforced, and seldom issue in concrete results. A common fate does hang over all those whose lives are governed by the state's decrees.

In so complicated a social system, even the organ of government cannot draw people together in common action toward the public good. The problem is not simply the natural tendencies, so to speak, of the industrial age, in which work becomes increasingly specialized, offices more formal, rules more complex, and action attenuated along the length of a chain of command that seems to have no definable beginning or end. The problem is also that the state perpetuates and enforces such complexity. The state preempts constructive action without taking enough initiative itself. The power to achieve united action requires conditions of less complexity and more freedom than the state, in modern societies, will provide. On the contrary, the complexity of work and politics in modern societies appears to call for further extensions of the state's own apparatus.

Take one of the most recent and saddening tragedies, the sudden explosion of toxic gas in Bhopal, India, in which over two thousand persons died, and two hundred thousand suffered painfully. This discussion of the events immediately after the disaster is hardly complete; it lacks an account of the process of litigation that was only beginning at the time of this writing. Many of the later news accounts seemed less richly detailed than the ones in the earliest reporting by *The New York Times*; in those, we have the specific and highly plausible statements of individuals whose shock, and whose failure to have imagined that such a disaster could occur, are far more useful than the later statements by various individuals and agents who were parties to the litigation.

At the very simplest level, we have here an example of devastation due to what Kropotkin called "the role of the state in the industrial field." In its study of the disaster in Bhopal, the *New York Times* discovered that the plant was poorly designed and unprofitable. It was poorly designed, because it was too big, ten times larger than any similar facility for producing methyl-isocyanate. The plant had had many flaws in its design as a result of its size, e.g. pumps and pipes that had to be replaced (*New York Times*, 3 February 1985, A6). In the recent years of its operation, the plant simply was too big in its productive capacity; it had been designed for a market that never developed. (ibid.) Instead, the plant became increasingly unprofitable: a drought reduced demand; government subsidies favored other products; government rules required continuous investment; and other pesticides at lower prices increased their share of the market at Union Carbide's expense. In short, two forces converged—human error, and capitalism as it operates in modern state.

A complex industrial order, in which conflict had to be managed according to the rites presided over by the state, made genuine solutions impossible and protracted certain problems until a disaster finally occurred. Because the plant was operating at a loss, repairs were not made to such vital safety features as towers, stacks, a crucial refrigerator and gauges. As the plant became unprofitable, workers were allowed to leave without being replaced, and their training, unsatisfactory from the outset, was further neglected. For over a year, "there had been six rather than twelve operators on a shift," and "there was a backlog of (unfilled) jobs" (*New York Times,* 28 January 1985, A6). Despite the fact that systems, absolutely necessary to prevent such an explosion as did occur on December 3, were not operating, the chief operating office of Union Carbide India, Ltd. reportedly said that the only cutbacks in equipment and personnel at the plant were merely an effort to reduce "avoidable and wasteful expenditures." (ibid.) What appeared to be a wasteful expenditure was, in fact, an essential protection against the fatal gassing of masses of workers and citizens. At this simplest level, of course, all those who become caught up in a capitalist economy share the same fate, that is, they are subject to more or less acceptable risks to ensure a continuous and reasonable return on capital investment.

Of course, there is more to the story than a question of profits and mass fatalities. The workers were merely "cogs in the administrative machine," as Kropotkin put it. One of the operators was Rahaman Khan, who had been ordered to flush out with water an improperly sealed pipe a few hours before the explosion. Water from that flushing may have been a catalyst in the eventual reaction; at the time of the first reports, the final analysis on the chemical reaction had not been made. What was then certain, however, was that both the operator and the supervisor who ordered the flushing of the pipe knew that valves could not be relied on to prevent leaks; they also knew that seals should be installed to prevent water from seeping through to the storage tanks. According to the *Times,* "Mr. Kahn said he knew the pipe was unsealed but 'it was not my job' to do anything about it" (28 January 1985, A7). Mr. Khan also knew that he was simply one cog among many in the industrial machine: "I was trained for one particular area and one particular job. I don't know about other jobs. During training they just said, 'These are the valves you are supposed to turn, this is the system in which you work, here are the instruments and what they indicate.' That's it" (ibid.). That is what it means to be a cog. Complexity becomes a form of domination in itself, but potential conflicts over the running of a plant are displaced to an administrative arena where they become lost in the state's regulations. A labyrinth keeps people confused and trapped, especially when it is built by the king.

There is clearly more at fault here than merely the quest for profits and the reduction of workers to cogs in an industrial process too complex for them to grasp; the state's regulatory agencies, designed to adjudicate conflicts and prevent disasters, had rites of their own. Consider the numerous inspectors whose job it was to guarantee the workers' and the public's safety. Not that the inspectors were numerous enough. Whereas the International Labor Organization recommends a ratio no smaller than one inspector for fifty workers in such an industry, according to the *New York Times* (31 January 1985, A8), there was about one inspector for one hundred fifty workers, and there were fifteen inspectors for 8,000 plants in Madhya Pradesh (ibid). Some of these inspectors, like the Bhopal plant's workers, were not adequately trained; the two inspectors in Bhopal assigned to the plant had degrees not in chemistry but in mechanical engineering and did not understand or concern themselves with what was being produced (ibid.).

The problem of the inspectors, however, was more severe than understaffing and inadequate training; they also lacked the authority to make a difference to the operation itself. Consider these items from the *New York Times'* account (ibid).

> The factory inspectors' job was limited to looking after safety devices to protect workers. "We do not design, maintain, and operate plants" (said one official in the state's labor department's division of industrial health and safety), "We only check to see there are enough protective masks and safety guards."

> Similarly, U.K. Tiwari, chairman of the pollution control board, said his agency lacked responsibility because methyl-isocyanate, called MIC, was *not a normal emission* of the factory and therefore was not monitored at all. Instead, he said, the factory's regular noxious emissions were "almost nothing."

> Inspectors have little authority to order that unsafe conditions be remedied, apart from going to court. That process often takes years and then the fines are minimal.

Those with the authority to give orders apparently lack the power to enforce them. One official had ordered the plant to move away from the area in which it was located in order to protect the citizens from precisely such an accident. The official, a Mr. M.N. Buch, "then commissioner and director of town and country planning for the state," had, in 1975, ordered the Carbide plant to find another location. The order was ignored, and Mr. Buch "soon after . . . took another job for unrelated reasons" (ibid., loc. cit.). The state's rituals could only encompass "normal" emissions: normalcy reigned. When the state, in order to prevent disaster, did issue an order, there was no way to disrupt the continuing process of complaint, inspection, report, and inaction by which normalcy continued to reign. Taken to extremes of complexity, the ritualization of conflict paralyzed even those whose authority depends on the prescribed performance of the rites.

On the one hand, the state preempts the authority to take remedial or constructive action on the behalf of the people themselves; the sheer fact of the state's presence makes it possible and necessary for the state to take action. On the other hand, the conditions for *effective* action require that individuals should be and feel responsible to one another, have ways of communicating and responding to each other, and have organs that ensure that those who take action are not only responsible but accountable. Collective action thus requires something more than the vacuum left by the expansion of the state at the expense of such mediating institutions as the press, the unions, universities, religious organizations, and other such organizations. The state causes the slow atrophy of these organs for collective action on which the state's own effectiveness eventually depends. In the ensuing vacuum, the state acts without effect or fails to act at all.

The state's role in the tragedy is slowly emerging in the accounts gleaned by reporters to the *New York Times*. Note, for instance, that "A Bhopal journalist, Raajkumar Keswani, had been warning of potential disaster at the plant in his now defunct Hindi weekly, "Rapat" (*New York Times* 31 January 1985, A8). The reports, supported by complaints from local unions representing workers at the plant, led to discussions in the state legislature on the twenty-first of December, 1982, nearly two years before the "accident." The press, unions, and the legislature were attempting to do the job of so-called mediating institutions, but according to the *New York Times* the state essentially quashed further discussion and debate of the issue. The Chief Minister of the State, Arjun Singh, was present at the debate, and so was the labor minister for the state, Mr. Tara Singh Viyogi, who reportedly stated to the legislature: "Mr. Speaker, this plant was established here in 1969 with an investment of 250 million rupees ($20 million at current rates). It is not a small piece of stone that I can shift from one place to another." He added, "there is no danger to the city, nor do I find any symptoms of it." Mr. Viyogi, now a textile labor union leader in Gwalior, about 200 miles north of Bhopal, denied in an interview any responsibility for the accident. It seems that Mr. Viyogi thought that everything would be safe as long as the instruments worked properly. Mr. Viyogi was perhaps unaware that there had been a fatal accident at the plant a year before the public debate (ibid.). In any event, his failure was indeed due to lack of imagination: "I never imagined it," he said. "It was beyond my thinking that it could happen" (ibid.). Although the press, labor unions, and the legislature thought the matter debatable and sounded alarmed, the state was not stimulated to creative thinking or action. Such is the vacuum, in which no one can operate except through the rituals of the state—rituals designed to minimize conflict and to forestall terrible disruptions.

The state's mind may well have boggled at its own complexities, let alone the complexities of instrument panels and chemical chain reactions. The central government had licensed the plant and delegated to the state of Madhya Pradesh the responsibility of monitoring the plant under four national laws, but the *New York Times* chronicles a long list of local and state officials who could have taken action to prevent the disaster, had they known of the chemical's potential hazard to the community or simply acted on the various reports of accidents and safety hazards at the plant: the chief minister, Arjun Singh, and Mr. Tiwari who regarded the plant's noxious emissions as "almost nothing"; the labor minister; the chief inspector of factories who allegedly "renewed the factory's license annually without acting on reports of safety lapses from the labor department"; the state's director of public health; the mayor of Bhopal; the chief administrative officer for the district; and the chief of police (ibid.).

The complexity of a modern division of labor is itself difficult enough to grasp without being aggravated, reinforced, intensified, and perpetuated by the complex apparatus of the state. Given sufficient complexity, positive action dies a slow death. Some had no information. Others had the information but lacked the responsibility to act on it; like the chief minister they thought local officials and plant managers "most closely concerned" had the greater responsibility. Some with the responsibility to act lacked the authority; it was the job of another official in another department, perhaps, to take the requisite action. Some with the authority lacked the will or the imagination; they could not conceive of what might happen. That, indeed, is how all come to share a common fate: complexity framed by an organization that preempts but fails to take collective action while eroding the ability of others to unite and act on their own behalf.

Of course, there are other factors at play in the Bhopal tragedy. Capitalism may be either incompatible with any undeveloped area or concomitantly more dangerous; I am simply arguing that, *within the framework of the state,* capitalism causes an area to remain undeveloped by stifling that area's own forms of production for its own needs while fostering production for the needs of stockholders, foreign investors, and distant markets. It certainly appears that Indian industry is at the mercy of foreign capital, and that Indian management is not sufficiently independent of foreign owners. Union Carbide in the United States had insisted, over the objections of its Indian subsidiary, on stockpiling large quantities of the fatal chemical, far more than were actually needed to meet the requirements of production (*Wall Street Journal,* 2/5/85:2). The Indian management reportedly objected that the supplies were neither needed nor safe, but American management prevailed. The stockpiles, excessive even for production in the United States, were created and kept both in Bhopal and at the plant site in West Virginia. The relative balance of power between owners and managers or between Indian and American corporate officials, of interest to those who apply abstract models of economic systems to specific situations, may also interest those engaged in litigation resulting from the tragedy. It would also be important to know how cohesive is the capitalist class in both countries and to decide whether management is more or less a part of the class of owners. One might also ask whether an industry like Union Carbide is trying to maximize profits or simply guarantee a satisfactory rate of return. Here, however, I am simply asking how social complexity and the ritualization of conflict through the state keeps people mystified, passive, and unable to unite for effective action in their common interests. How does the state ritualize conflict in a social system already too elaborate to be easily controlled? I have been suggesting that the state gives the appearance of order, fairness, and legitimacy to a social system that is itself out of popular control and in the hands of a more or less cohesive élite.

The state, as this abstract and repressive framework, reassures that normalcy will prevail and that life, therefore, will go on. The *New York Times,* reporting on the people living nearest the factory, interviewed many who said that they never dreamed that the factory would be a source of fatal gas. On the contrary, they heard alarms, but thought the alarms were routine. Even the most militant and active leaders of the local community assumed that the often-heard alarms at the factory were for the workers; the bells tolled not for them. Like the state labor minister, they never "imagined" that such a disaster could take place; it was "beyond" their thinking. To ritualize conflict through the state has the effect of any ritual; it captures the imagination and protects it from death-anxiety.

Such a lack of imagination is one clear sign of repression; in fact, Herbert Read (1974:72) borrows from Freud to make this very point. Social repression pushes disruptive wishes and fears into the unconscious, where they live a half-life and are unavailable as the sources of energy or impetus to common action. Of course, Read is speaking particularly of the dullness of the English citizen's imagination when he speaks about the average individual's fear of being different, abnormal, even artistic; instead, the English accept routine, put up with an "absolute poverty of ideas," ridicule the eccentric, ape the gentry, and seek at all costs to preserve the smooth flow of social life with an untroubled facade (1954:72–73). What Read said of the English has more general application and might well be said of the officials, managers, and workers who suppressed their own fears and alarms by tending to their own business routines. As Read put it, this is "the neurosis of normality" (1954:71).

In view of the apathy of the ruled, some anarchists, like Emma Goldmann, have spoken bitterly of "the masses"—their inertia and their willingness to submit to rulers, to place their destiny in the hands of others; she speaks of their "craveness" (1969:70–71). More understanding, perhaps, Read explains the popular willingness to trust appearance, to go along, and to believe that their fate is in good hands by "a blind unconscious identification of (with) the leader and the father and by the inhibited instincts which alone make such an identification possible" (1954:96). It is indeed a failure of the imagination to believe that the state would never license a plant that could be lethal for those who live nearby, but that failure stems from repression and from the desire to acquire the protection and the (imagined or real) powers of those in authority. Inertia is in this way a symptom, like normalcy, of devotees of the cult of authority.

Were it not for the desire to be secure and for the resulting tendency to submit to a higher power, the state could not preempt a central place in the cult of authority. Through its several agencies, offices, laws, regulations, and personnel, however, the state encourages, intensifies and perpetuates attitudes ranging from reverence, through servility, to passivity.

There is a great deal of hatred for the powers that be in any cult, just as there is a great deal of hatred for the father in the heart of the son, repressed, of course, but nonetheless active. Where an anarchist might simply find a passive desire to submit to authority and to be protected, Freud would add one further element, a desire for punishment to assuage the individual's guilt for having hated the father or having tried to take his place and so remove him from his rightful position of authority. "A great need for punishment develops in the ego, which in part offers itself as a victim to fate . . . Even fate is, in the last resort, only a later father-projection" (1963:283). That is why the anarchist program calls for the revolt of the child against the father: it is part of the revolt against oneself.

Repression in a modern society comes in part from the willing habituation of individuals and groups to a complex social order. It comes in part from the state, and makes such complexity less threatening and more manageable, just as it makes habituation to being dominated a moral and political obligation. Finally, repression stems from the desire for the father's protection and the desire, in the end, for punishment for the real or imagined sin of having taken the father's place. Only a courageous demand for independence will free the individual from a subservience born of the need for protection and of habituation to an increasingly complex division of social life into agencies and occupations. Ultimately, the achievement of that independence necessitates the dissolution of the political institutions that make habituation necessary and reinforce domination through complexity. Once dissolved, the state will no longer provide the context for a rational belief in a common fate.

It is no wonder, then, that the anarchist turns to heroes for examples of individuals who manage to break through the barriers to imagination and so become their own fathers—independent, self-sustaining, creative, and yet not so individualistic that they fail to carry with them the concerns of their own people. Read draws heavily on Freud's discussion of the epic poet who, casting his father in the form of a monster, slays the beast and achieves for himself both independence from the group and freedom from the father's control. In the same context, Read (1954:97) assails communist apologists who cynically adopt Freud's analysis of the individual's yearning for the father to take advantage of the masses' need for authoritative leadership. In contrast to this manipulative social engineering, Read argues, the anarchist "comes of age; he disowns the father; he lives in accordance with his own ego-ideal. He becomes conscious of his individuality" (ibid.:97). The heroic individual leaves, once and for all, the cult of authority.

Frankly, I do not share these hopes for the epic poet. The task of the hero is to kindle the collective imagination, to simplify a complex world, to point to a unity that fails to bring oppression, and so kindle the spirits of the vast majority that they prefer an open-ended, spontaneous, and vital existence to a common fate (cf. Berger 1975:68). But even Read knows that the modern artist, like any modern worker, can be reduced to a cog in the machine. Modern artists, then, may decorate public spaces but they lack a popular vision and have no popular base; instead, they become increasingly innovative and complex in a social vacuum (Read 1954:226–28).

Read's heroes are sometimes an odd choice. On the one hand, he understandably points to Gandhi whose individual vision had collective roots and pointed toward a common future that presumably would allow individuals to pursue their own several and separate fates (1954:215–16). Among his other heroes, however, Samoans and Americans rather strangely appear as pioneers of another sort—epic heroes of the anarchist's or anthropologist's imagination. Here he draws on the work of Margaret Mead, whose accuracy has recently become more controversial; and he shares Mead's vision of Americans as "committed to the importance of freedom that comes by knowledge and understanding rather than from coercion, fixed authority, or final revelation" (1954:218). The choice of Americans is strange, not only because others might describe Americans as far more easily coerced, subservient to authority, and entranced by at least a biblical revelation; it is also strange because Read himself finds the ultimate guarantor of a liberating imagination in an eternal source of illumination that is immutable and universal (1954:106–8). How can a pluralistic and secular society, committed to change and to endless innovation, pursue a truth that is liberating, universal, and indubitably real? Anarchist thought, even when it is conscious of its own paradoxes, still tries to root innovation in what is eternal, individual liberty in communal solidarity, equality in elitist visions of the truth. In a secular society, however, there is no substitute for a direct attack on social-structural complexity and on the rites by which conflict is avoided and perpetuated. That means, at the very least, a drastic reduction in the size and scope of the state and in the level of complexity. The elaborate codification of modern societies exceeds the scope of our imagination, although at times of tragedy, such as the one at Bhopal, individuals can begin to grasp how that complexity does create a common fate that binds those who prosper with those who suffer and die.

The bond, as Lifton (1976) points out, may be a bond of mutual guilt among those who survive, a bond of remorse and of shared responsibility that makes a common fate seem even desirable. In a secular society, however, even obligations to the dead will not weigh so heavily on the living.

Here I have focussed primarily on the state as the primary institution barring progress to a more secular society. The state gathers its support partly on the basis of the complexity of social life; no doubt some agency must seek to order, if not wholly to control, the extraordinary range and variety of ideas, goods, and services exchanged within and among nations. However, the authority conferred on the state to provide unity in the midst of complexity creates a barrier to free and constructive solutions to problems and conflicts arising from production. The sheer presence of the state displaces other forms of activity without taking constructive political action. The state licenses or ignores the industries whose products become potentially lethal, while those living under the authority of the state come to believe that they are living under its protection. Only certain actions, products, goods, services and even ideas find outlets, and these are the ones to which the state has no objection. The generalization applies to the transfer of technology for producing pesticides and to the free association of citizens who seek to emigrate or claim asylum. The desire to avoid conflict and disruption leads to the ritualization presided over by the state, whose authority derives from the desire to control an increasingly complex and intimidating social system. The cult of political sovereignty will remain until there is a widespread moral, social, and economic exodus from the state itself.

The conditions for such an exodus become more favorable as a global economy imposes burdens and conflicts, which the nation-state cannot resolve. Giddens has noted that:

> In the world capitalist economy, which by the nineteenth century had already become a genuinely global system, the main connections over a broad territorial scale are economic; politico-military power is in the hands of nation-states, each of which has strictly delimited territories of jurisdiction (1982:146).

A global economy requires international responses to problems and to tragedy, but a nation-state provides only a limited, local arena for ritualizing conflict. Tragedies such as the disaster of Bhopal bind populations together across national boundaries; one nation's grievances must be satisfied in another nation's courts, and the solution sought through one another's generosity and ingenuity. There is, however, no *national* solution to the problem of poisonous gasses emitted from the chimneys of industries like Union Carbide, just as there is no *national* solution to the acid rain that kills life without respect to national boundaries. The state is like an obsessive neurosis: a compartmentalized area of a person's life in which the individual seeks subjective, partial, and temporary solutions to problems that encompass one's whole life and would link the individual, if one allowed oneself the privilege, to a larger community of human suffering and experience. There is no hope for a solution to global problems through such rigidly compartmentalized social units as the nation-state. The anarchist agenda calls for an assertion of historical imagination and will: i.e., the commitment to destroy that which stands in the way, precisely so that new social conditions can stimulate new forms of social imagination.

The nation-state was derived from the very sentiments that will eventually call for its dissolution. As Giddens notes, the nation-state itself had many sources: the increased ability to turn industry to military uses, the extraordinary advances in communication and transportation that helped unify the administration of larger territories, and the eventual amalgamation of over five hundred European political units into twenty-five by 1900 (1982:162–63); the source of the nation-state's *authority*, however, lay in nationalism, a set of loyalties by which individuals in a given area claimed to be members of the same linguistic, religious, moral, and eventually political community (ibid.:163). Not all nation-states enjoy the support of these sentiments, and of course the formation of the states profited from the destruction of smaller communities; the relation between nationalism and the rise of the nation-state is neither peaceful nor perfect. The point is that the nation-state, by its monopoly of force and the sheer destructiveness of its policies and weapons, creates ever-widening bonds of solidarity that eventually reach far beyond national borders. In the Second World War, Read notes, "the deepest emotions were stirred, not by purely military operations, but by the bombing of open towns, by the massacre of women and children, by the enslavement of whole races" (1954:207–8). He goes on to note, and for our discussion this is a crucial point, that the nations have not been able to profit from the emotions of solidarity they have aroused among people across national boundaries; the common fund is there, and it cannot readily be exploited for reasons of state. A presidential visit to a cemetery cannot only provide a gesture of international reconciliation but embarrass and thwart the administration. It is not yet clear whether the nation can successfully reduce the common bonds of people offering one another mutual aid to loyalties to their separate states. I propose that the most common and powerful sentiments uniting people in their work and suffering will be lost in any such nationalist translation.

4

Education and the Cult of Authority: Ritualizing Conflict Between the Classes and Between Generations

A WHOLLY SECULAR SOCIETY lacks any major conflict between the generations because the present is not beholden to the past. That is what it means to be secular, in one sense of the term: passing away, temporal. Another sense of the term comes close to the first: epochal, of an era. "Secular" progress concerns the present age or time, and in a foreshortened sense, secular progress may be merely a brief trend or cycle. In both uses of the term, secular means for the time being, an indefinite time, bounded really by the death of one generation or the next. The past loses its hold over the present as the current generation disowns any debt to the previous generations. The "dead hand" of the past is lifted, and the reign of dead persons' values comes to an end.

The idea of a secular society can therefore be utopian, since it heralds the end of that perennial conflict between generations that no society has yet fully prevented or cured. The utopian aspect of the idea was once—and perhaps best—expressed by an English sectarian, William Godwin, who had been brought up in a millenarian religious tradition in the eighteenth century and was therefore no stranger to ideas of a radical departure from the past. As in most millenarian thought, there are dramatic reversals in Godwin's scheme: reversals of common sense and of the ordinary course of events. Some think of social life as a world apart from nature, where freedom prevails, whereas nature is supposedly governed by some determinism; Godwin, however, finds that social life, "artificial" and "arbitrary" though it is, becomes a source of necessity rather than of freedom, because individuals are governed by the past and by past experience. Secular societies, however, offer the reverse; individuals will declare their freedom from the past and so exercise their will quite freely. Whatever determines their choices will be the intrinsic goodness or rightness of the design or object of their plans (cf. Woodcock 1962:71–72).

As Woodcock points out, Godwin's ideas on politics represent a secularized version of the English dissenting tradition in religion. He is distrustful of all government because it

> gives substance and permanence to our errors (and) prompts us to seek the public welfare, not in innovation and improvement, but in a timid reverence for the decisions of our ancestors, as if it were the nature of mind always to degenerate and never to advance. (In *An Account of the Seminary*, 1784, quoted in Woodcock, 1962:75)

His hostility to government, then, is based on his desire to overcome the weight of authority invested in previous generations and their values. His passion for freedom leads him to declare government an exercise in subordination not only to rulers but to the past itself. Only the future can be the source and object of the free exercise of the will and of the imagination (cf. Woodcock ibid.:72). One can hear in Godwin the later, more familiar theme of Karl Marx on prose, as the language of the past; the language of the future can only be poetry. In the conclusion of this chapter, we will return to the thought of Herbert Read, whose own paeans to individual freedom recall Godwin's of two centuries ago. The point here, of course, is that as a millenarian sect committed to the idea of a secular society, anarchism can find salvation only in the future. In a secular society, conflict between generations is literally a thing of the past.

In this chapter, I assume that the conflict between generations is still endemic even to modern, only partially secularized, societies. The millenium has not come, in which the generations succeed each other without conflict. On the contrary, that conflict remains, although it has been displaced from its primary setting, the home, to a wide range of other contexts, such as the school, the workplace, and the political party. Here we will focus on education as one locus, and perhaps the most important one, for analyzing the way in which generational conflict has been ritualized.

Of course, that conflict is not only displaced to the schools but transformed into symbols. Education is more than the mere transmission or acquisition of symbols; there is always a sense in which those symbols represent an inheritance from the past that is presented to each new generation as a legacy that imposes certain rights and obligations. Conflict ensues over what the new generation must do with the symbols to acquire those rights and discharge those obligations. The so-called "inflation" in grades is merely one indicator of a shift in the balance of power between successive generations. No doubt education also organizes and presents these symbols at levels of abstraction higher with each grade in school. The objects of the educational exercise become more difficult to locate in concrete terms either in the world of ideas or under the microscope. The rewards for apprehending these abstractions also become increasingly abstract, as merit becomes defined and redefined according to various professions' criteria for mastery. Children are sorted and tracked, and in the end they are learning some aspect of what a particular guild, occupation, or type of work recognizes as the symbols under its control. In the same process, the authorities become increasingly distant and the object of greater respect, but their transcendence of the student's personal experience makes them the object of considerable distrust as well as veneration. The most distant and respected authorities, of course, are members of previous generations and are usually dead. It goes without saying that, when measured by these criteria, the individual's own insight and experience become increasingly insignificant until the student has been certified as an heir to an occupational or intellectual tradition, at which point the significance of individual effort begins to return. In the meantime, the individual is reduced to a member of a category, i.e., of a class, often numbered by the years spent in school or eventually by the year of graduation. These supraindividual designators are reminders of the relative weight of previous generations, just as the super individual status of the "masters" gives them more authority than a merely logical or empirical analysis of their work might warrant. To be charged with inconsistency and contradiction does not seriously weaken the claims on behalf of the masters; the same charges can drastically lower the grade of the aspiring student. The system is complex, but its process of ritualizing conflict is the one with which we are familiar.

Before embarking on a more careful discussion of how generational conflict is ritualized in education, I wish to point to one way in which individuals become "dupes of the social system." Ritualizing intergenerational conflict in the schools does result in a form of deception carried out by competent and well-intentioned parents, students, teachers, administrators, and by more distant authorities who support the school system. Here are some examples of how these interests operate surreptitiously. First, there is the interest of the teacher, who controls curriculum design and notions of human development that are not entirely accessible either to the students or their families. There are other authorities in the community who also have an interest in controlling the behavior of the young—those who control the command-systems of work and of politics, for instance. The interests of particular occupational groups appear in various lesson plans, as children are taught what others do for a living; the interests of the state appear in lessons about the police or the political system. Through these several authorities and their interests runs the class-system in all its complexity. No wonder that critics of education speak of the "hidden curriculum" or, as I shall point out in the next section of this chapter, of an "invisible pedagogy." By displacing and translating social conflict from the home or the streets into the classroom, any society virtually ensures that the substance of that conflict will be transformed and therefore disguised.

Organizations like the school or, for that matter, like any corporation, are always more or less "authentic" or "inauthentic." Etzioni (1968) has suggested the use of these terms to mark the distance between an organization's stated and actual objectives, and I take that suggestion here in discussing schools. The stated objectives of any educational institution seldom stress the particular interests of the community or of the state in social control or of particular occupational groups in perpetuating their monopolies over particular kinds of work and information. Seldom does an educational institution state that its objective is to reproduce the prevailing class relationships in the larger society. It takes very little sophistication to know, however, that educational institutions do produce citizens and, while allowing mobility for certain individuals, preserve distinctions between classes. Very few schools challenge the monopoly of an occupational group over the ownership and control of certain kinds of work and information. Such objectives would be inconsistent, in fact, with the task of accomodating a new generation to the authority of previous generations. By introducing a new generation to its inheritance, the schools also pass on a number of hindrances to the free play and development of individual capacities. These are commonplace observations, of course, but I state them here as a reminder of the cost of ritualizing social conflict. The cost, borne by a wide range of social institutions, is a certain lack of authenticity.

Rituals in the Education System

Rituals are exercises performed at the borders: the border between one country and another, between one stage of life and the next, or even between one social status and another. At the border of a country one must successfully perform certain formalities before one is allowed to cross the threshhold. As one moves from one stage in life to the next, for instance, from adolescence to adulthood, one must cross certain borders or threshholds before one is allowed to drink, or to marry, or to kill. To ensure that those who pass over the threshhold are properly prepared, societies provide certain rites to subdue, purify, transform, and ennoble those who are allowed to pass. Certainly, as one approaches a person of a higher social status one approaches an invisible barrier or threshhold between persons of different authority in an organization or of different standing in the community.

Some need to be reminded of the ceremonies that facilitate the crossing of these boundaries; the forgetful will usually be reminded that they have failed to make the proper gestures of acquiescence and obedience. Sometimes these boundaries have physical markers—a title on the door, a bar before the judge's bench, a rail before the altar, or merely a proper distance between those who speak from different "levels" in the community. The literature on rites of passage is by now so complex that it needs a separate introduction simply to chart the shoals and learn the technical terminology (cf. Van Gennep 1960; Huntington and Metcalf 1979; Turner 1969). *The point of these rites is to prevent something terrible from happening: to avoid a temptation or to forestall a disaster.* That "something," of course, is often conflict between generations or members of different classes. To ignore these rituals in social life can therefore be dangerous.

The obsessive who performs certain magical rites does so to avoid anguish. These rites soften the pain of hatred or remorse, and the pangs of love; they reduce life to manageable, and neurotic, proportions. In the same way, social rituals also minimize the human pain that comes from being fully exposed to the lives of others. The anguish of individuals who face starvation, torture, or other forms of subjugation is overwhelming; borders between classes or countries provide a partial insulation against the suffering of others. Those who cross these borders still face various forms of quarantine until they can be purified and transformed into people who can be trusted not to disturb the prevailing distribution of happiness and misery.

To move from one stage in life to the next also imposes some obligations on those on both sides of the imaginary social barrier between generations. Those moving up must say goodbye to parts of themselves and to some ways of life that have been useful or even precious; they must also pass some tests that can be frighteningly severe. Those on the other side of the generational border must also face exposure to the insecurity, ambition, or carelessness of those who represent new competition for relatively scarce places of authority. The cult of authority, whose rituals these are, requires a sacrifice of intellect or of the most intrusive sorts of ambition.

Finally, those who approach individuals of a higher or lower status will feel various sorts of pain if they are at all vulnerable to others' suffering or pretensions. Jonathan Kozol borrows Paul Goodman's phrase, "Sunday afternoon neurosis," to describe the absentminded and fainthearted twilight world in which students and teachers discuss suffering, evil, and death. Like other critics, Kozol stresses the use of language to disguise the reality of others' pain and of one's own responsibility for that pain; language also provides a way of covering one's own feelings of abhorrence and shame for one's complicity in others' suffering. For instance, in discussing the substitution of the word "waste" by the military for "kill," Kozol goes on to argue that such linguistic formulae originate in a classroom where all forms of suffering are regarded as "problems" or "dilemmas" to be solved or managed by the application of appropriate technology or by the introduction of democratic processes. It is this use of language to provide an artificial barrier between others and oneself that keeps obligations from being immediate and specific.

The classroom becomes a place where insulation against others' pain—and against one's own—depends on a lack of interruption: an orderly and continuous series of exchanges between teachers and students and an equally orderly and continuous progress from one part of the curriculum to the next. Just as an obsessive's defenses against pain depend on getting things right in an orderly fashion, so in the classroom interruption can give pain an opportunity to intervene.

The price of normalcy is not only an incomplete grasp of one's own emotional life but of the joy and suffering of others. Jonathan Kozol expresses it simply enough by quoting Cesar Chavez's comment that "to be a man, is to suffer for others" (1980:54). Kozol argues that the classroom provides a substitute for genuine experience, including the experience of suffering for oneself or others; the substitute comes to take the place of the real thing and to confuse the adult about reality itself. If an individual speaks and gestures in ways that require a drastic reduction of personal experience and perception, that adult is clearly in the grip at least of a neurosis. Social life, by the same argument, is no less pathological for offering more legitimate barriers to experience and perception.

Some of these barriers are the social rituals which make proximity to other human beings less frightening, less open to surprise and conflict, and potentially therefore less painful. A ritual allows the participants to continue acting in a "normal" fashion, as if they were not vulnerable and as if no interruption in their lives had occurred. Just as an obsessive goes through motions without interruption in order to prevent some emotional disturbance from developing, the routines of the classroom or the office serve the same obsessive function of forestalling painful disruption. It is the characteristic of ritual to make it possible to act as if nothing untoward has happened or will happen. The rules of polite intercourse will be observed, and no one will be hurt.

Given the necessity to act as if there is a place for everyone and as if everyone is in their place, a ritual must continue if it is to be successful; it must continue, furthermore, in precisely the right order: first grade, second grade; soup, salad; confession, absolution; election, inauguration; exchange of rings and vows, then the pronouncement of the clergy that the couple is married; the cessation of heartbeat and brainwave, and only then the doctor's pronouncement that death has occurred. To reverse or interrupt a ritual is to allow the unexpected and threatening to occur. If one can sit through the ritual as it is performed in proper sequence from beginning to end, one can presumably go through life to the end without flinching and without pain or disbelief. Kozol notes:

> Acquiescence in the face of *sequence* in and of itself—this is the final and most remorseless means by which we demonstrate our willingness to forgo reservations and withhold dissent. No matter what we

do or say, in individual classes or in isolated moments *during* those
twelve years, the fact that we have stuck it out in relative silence for
one sixth of our entire life, this in itself is primary evidence, for
those who need to know, that we have been correctly trained to
permanent abnegation of our own beliefs (1980:20).

In political parlance the exhortation to "stay the course" has
mobilized a certain consent in the American electorate precisely
because the phrase falls on ears made receptive by careful training
not to interrupt the curriculum. Just as rituals preserve symbolic
boundaries between individuals and groups who might otherwise
be competitive or dangerous to one another, ritual also provides
insurance against the premature withdrawal of consent from
social policies or from regimes whose effects become increasingly
painful over time.

The need to interrupt the smooth surface of social life is a
primary tenet of the anarchist credo for precisely the reasons
already given: that the sequence of appropriate words and deeds
protects the powerful, gives legitimacy to the current distribution
of authority, and exacts continuing contributions from those who
must make the weekly offering or pay the annual tax to support
the system in question. To interrupt a social process is precisely
necessary if one is to stop these sacrifices and challenge legitimate
authority. That is why, for instance, blacks in the 1960s or steel
workers in the 1980s have found it necessary to disrupt liturgies in
the congregations of affluent Americans. Blacks poured the wine
of communion on the chancel carpet to dramatize the very real
sacrifices being exacted by the class system outside of Church;
steel workers more recently sought to make their point by inter-
rupting the flow of liturgical words in the congregations of suburban Pittsburgh. Jonathan Kozol (1980) tells the story of waiting
with one of his students, an epileptic, in a metropolitan hospital's
emergency room; the nurse in charge of the room insisted that
procedures be followed in a proper sequence that consisted of
filling out forms and waiting for one's turn. A few hours—and
four painful seizures—later, Kozol simply took a doctor by the
arm and led him to the patient who, after an injection, was
immediately restful once again. The cruelty of "staying the
course" could hardly have been more graphically illustrated. The
anarchist proposal requires that one speak out of turn and in
terms that are uncalled for by the rules of the church or classroom
or court.

On the one hand, the smooth and orderly progression of

speakers and topics in social life ensures that nothing untoward or terrible will happen; the rituals of social life, like those of the obsessive, ward off the danger of unfamiliar or surprising intrusions into the life and consciousness of those who prefer to follow the appropriate sequence to the very end. On the other hand, it is precisely this preference for sequence that leads to disaster: another seizure in the hospital waiting room; another worker in despair; another child malnourished, sickly, or dead.

What angers Kozol about the ritualized transactions of modern societies is the same sense of perpetuating past error and of making it sacred that results "not in innovation and improvement," as Godwin put it in the passage quoted at the beginning of this chapter, but in "a timid reverence for the decisions of our ancestors." Kozol speaks of the imaginary connections that link the privileged children in a suburban school with those who despair in ghetto schools; Becker (1975) speaks of the pretense at connection made through ritualized ceremonies and spectacles in modern societies or through the habitual observance of common forms. Just as the school children imagine that they have done something effective through making contact with a legislator, the modern citizen, according to Becker, exercises a pretense at control through the rituals of modern government. The same "decadence of ritual," as Becker (1975) puts it, ensures that magical thinking will take the place of genuine innovation as individuals think that they have done something by manipulating a few symbols or engaging in the gestures of modern politics. Just as ritual perpetuates a reverence for institutions, even these habitual gestures will reinforce the citizen's obligation to the system; indeed Kozol and Becker know that the gestures express and perpetuate a sense of moral obligation to preserve the framework that provides for various inequities and establishes precedent in education or politics.

In this way, individuals assuage a sense of guilt that they may otherwise feel for having been too advantaged, and too protected from the sufferings of those overburdened by poverty or crushed by the state. Like Kafka's hero, Joseph K., the individual relieves guilt by discovering that others, too, share the same fate, and wait for the sentencing of an invisible judge. To ritualize social life is to guarantee that a common fate awaits all despite their present misfortune or most fortunate circumstances. To leave behind such a doctrine of predestination or necessity opens the way both to an attack on inequity and to a will genuinely freed from the operation of repressed, and therefore unconsciously operative, motives.

To revolt against such a culture, of course, is like tilting against windmills; the object of one's attack is notably resistant but difficult to locate in a fixed position. Nowhere is that resistance more apparent, of course, than among those who have a vested interest in transmitting the culture. That is why some of the most telling statements of the revolt against culture have recently come from intellectuals who attack educational institutions in their respective countries.

For instance, Kozol (1975; 1980) argues that public and private education in America falsely claims to open up to the student a wide array of moral and intellectual choices, whereas, in fact, education closes off discussion precisely at points strategic to the maintenance of the prevailing system of privilege. In the same vein, Marcuse (1968) has argued that culture in the West is one dimensional; in fostering an apparently open discussion on a wide range of topics it forecloses discussion of moral or political options that, if pursued, could lead to the transformation of a particular society.

In the very act of transmitting a culture, therefore, any institution, acting as the voice of reason, designates what is considered feasible, reasonable, pertinent, just, fair, and open to discussion. Take, for example, every list of moral, emotional, or intellectual steps that has been generated in the United States over the last generation of scholarship and inquiry into moral and human development. The most widely disseminated and easily criticized list is perhaps Kubler-Ross's widely accepted but truncated notion of "steps" in the "dying process": steps that presumably lead through denial and despair to the "acceptance" of death. In this way, the process by which one generation makes room for another can be ritualized. More sophisticated, but not less truncated, is Erikson's (1978) list of the "stages" in life. Inevitably, if all goes well, these "stages" lead to integrity and to wisdom; if developmental processes are frustrated and the individual fails to resolve earlier conflicts, of course, the individual will experience stagnation and despair: a recurrence of what Lifton reminds us are preoccupations at every stage in life, e.g., a need for connection, integrity, and a sense of movement. Perhaps more sacrosanct are Kohlberg's stages of moral development or Piaget's notions of cognitive development; both attempt to provide a model for ritualizing the transmission and acquisition of culture. But in ritualizing that transmission, however, whatever is liberating in a culture becomes a way of inducing successive generations to undertake obligations while acquiring their rights. Kozol's protest is a poignant one; he speaks of Lawrence Kohlberg as,

> an intelligent and influential man who has given years of research to the question of the evolution of a sense of "moral reason" in an adult or child. Even with all seeming dedication, Kohlberg cannot hold back from the use of the protective filter offered him by slots and numbers. People exist, as he reports with absolute certitude within his work, in one of six moral boxes: People are "LEVEL SIX" or "LEVEL ONE" or "LEVEL THREE" (1975, 1980:57).

It does not matter whether one agrees with Kohlberg on the content of a particular level; it is the very ordering itself that hints at the effort of the society to ritualize the process by which one generation succeeds another. Let us return, for a moment, to Kubler-Ross's well-known list of stages in dying. Granted that Dr. Kubler-Ross herself does not take the items in this list to be definitive, inevitable, or even orderly; many lesser practitioners have come to "know" that the approach to dying begins with "denial," passes through "anger," "depression," and "bargaining," and ends, if all goes well, in "acceptance." That leaves out Dylan Thomas's rage at the dying of the light; it also leaves out Christian joy and thanksgiving. Dr. Kubler-Ross's stages call for another and rather banal form of progress toward "acceptance" in a framework that excludes the most profound passions. Applied to the victims of Auschwitz, of which Dr. Kubler-Ross is a survivor, these stages make tragic sense. Applied to "all sorts of conditions" of human beings, they provide another means by which the worst of pain and suffering can be short-lived and somehow transcended rather than endured faithfully to the end, or overcome in triumph. A preoccupation with getting things right, with doing things in just the right way, in decency, and in order is suitable for the performance of a ritual: not suitable for a single effective act of defiance, of seizing control, of conquering an environment, or of changing the order of things. Like a ritual, these "stages" have a sequence, and it becomes incumbent on the living as well as on the dying to follow that sequence in the right order through to the final stage; otherwise those who impose the ritual will be frustrated if the catechumens leave in the middle, interrupt the sequence, or fail to say "Amen." The service is performed partly for the benefit of those who consent to go through the proper sequence, but the service also benefits those in the "service professions" who prescribe these various rituals for their patients, their clients, and their students.

Responsibility for education, therefore, is usually entrusted to those who guarantee that a society will proceed smoothly from one generation to the next. The attempt to educate children to become bearers of a free spirit and an enlightened conscience encounters many obstacles: the teacher's own interests in maintaining order and claiming esoteric knowledge; the parents' interests in maintaining or improving their children's class position; and the interests of future employers in shaping personalities who will fit neatly either into relatively narrow or hierarchical roles, or roles that require more adaptability, flexibility and entrepreneurship. There are many ways to express the disappointment in such truncated expectations for freedom and enlightenment through education; here I turn from the American accounts offered by Jonathan Kozol to Basil Bernstein's description of schools in England.

Like Kozol, Bernstein argues that schools appear to be open to individual variations when they are, in fact, relatively closed. Bernstein (1977) notes how teachers in the preschool (or infant school) movement in England fostered the play of children; their goal was to provide an apparently open and supportive climate in which the children's unique capabilities could become more visible and productive as the child reacted to the environment of the school. As Bernstein notes, "the concept basic to the invisible pedagogy is play . . . (which) adumbrates future 'doings' " and so reveals what the child is ready to do in the present (1977:120–21). In this Eden, however, there are several sources of corruption, all of which stem from the claim of the teacher to a certain unique authority. While the child is "playing," of course, the teacher is evaluating the child's abilities and level of development. This is hardly a free environment, especially since the teacher alone knows the criteria for assessing the child. Unless parents have been reading someone like Piaget, Bernstein notes, they may be hard put to challenge the teacher's assessment, and the child is kept under the illusion that it is the child, not the teacher, who is the judge of what she herself is doing. The teacher acts "*as if* the acquirer (child) is the source of the criteria" by which the acquirer's (child's) play is evaluated (Bernstein, 1977:119). The teacher maintains authority by providing the framework within which the child pursues certain options.

There is nothing inherently wrong with the fact that play can serve productive ends; the problem arises when certain constraints are placed on play, constraints that serve the ends of a specific order of which the teacher, for instance, is a representative and in which the teacher has a personal stake. Herbert Read is very clear about play. He unabashedly asserts the priority of play over work.

> There is no aspect of culture—language, war, science, art, or philosophy, not even religion—in whose evolution play does not enter as the creative factor. Play is freedom, is disinterestedness, and it is only by virtue of disinterested free activity that man has created his cultural values. Perhaps it is this theory of all work and no play that has made the Marxist such a very dull boy (1954:151–52).

So long as play must serve to foreshadow work, it can never be free; utilitarian play is a contradiction in terms. Only free play can serve ends that are truly useful to the evolution of the human community rather than only to those who own and control the means of symbolic production. Teachers are no exception to the rule that those in authority will perpetuate that authority. The rules governing play in the schools cannot foster disinterested play, precisely because specific interests have shaped those rules. Of course, the teacher's vested interest is only one among several that are less visible, perhaps, but more potent in the scope of their influence on what purports to be play in the schoolroom. The result is a deceptive and therefore inauthentic social order.

Bernstein's indictment of the movement to institutionalize play in the English schools rests on the fact that the teacher *appears* to surrender control, but actually retains control by setting a framework so broad, and by using criteria so abstract that the pedagogy is "invisible." While appearing to involve the child in acquiring an education, the teacher actually is engaging the child in reproducing the stages in a theory of development, each stage of which calls for particular pedagogical steps to be taken by teacher and student (Bernstein 1977:119–121). More severe is Bernstein's indictment of the totalitarian implications of the free school movement. While appearing to focus on particular developmental strategies, the teacher is surveying the whole child; it is the development of a person, not a pupil, that is sought in this pedagogy, a person who fits the model required by the teacher's chosen theory. As Bernstein puts it, this approach "implies a potentially all-embracing theory [that] gives rise to a total—but invisible surveillance" (1977:121). The cult of authority requires a careful examination of the heart and mind of the potential devotee.

A partially secularized society thus imposes many of the demands associated with far more traditional communities and ways of life. It is modern to focus on skills, training, abilities, and creative performances in order to foster development of a person who will be able to undertake highly specialized, demanding roles in a modern organization, where one is expected to be flexible, to adapt and create, to produce new ideas or objects rather than merely to reproduce yesterday's practices. On the surface, the movement toward freedom in the schools serves just such a pedagogical purpose and will foster the growth of a complementary personality. Below the surface, however, the child is being constrained by expectations no less specific and all encompassing than those in a small village or indeed in a religious community. The classroom becomes the seminary in which the ordinand is examined for evidence of the character suitable to one seeking ordination, for inclusion in the priesthood of all believers.

The sequences of everyday life are a form of induction into social worlds that lie well beyond the horizons of those engaged in a particular context and its prescribed gestures. Kozol finds the sequence of the curriculum an obligatory but mind-numbing set of steps that lead eventually to graduation. The graduates, however, are by the time of their leave-taking unable to engage in any acts of moral outrage. The sequences of the classroom, in his view, lead to acquiescence and quiescence in the face of untold and unnecessary human suffering. On Bernstein's (1977) view, however, the sequences of the classroom lead to one's induction into the class system itself. Although his discussion is worth considering in more detail, his point should be clear from the outset: the sequences of the classroom are, only on the surface, the rites of an independent institution; below the surface, however, these sequences are a set of steps that are determined by the requirements of another system, the economy, and are ordered according to the interests of certain classes that control the transmission and acquisition of culture. What appears, then, to be education is the reproduction of a class system; what appears to be learning is, in reality, a preparation for various roles in specific social strata. There is an undertow, in other words, that drags unwary bathers into the greater depths of the ocean even as they go through the motions of one stroke or another. While thinking they are making progress, they become increasingly distant from the shore and beyond their depth until it is too late. That is why a highly ritualized social life, where sequences are smooth and orderly, may be pathological in its consequences.

Of course, not even the rituals of the educational system are capable entirely of glossing over the underlying conflicts in a society. Bernstein disavows any notion that education merely reproduces the requirements of a particular class system for managers and workers of certain types. There is only a "broad correspondence" between the way individual students learn their lesson, and workers or managers do their jobs; there are also "apparent contradictions" between the rules governing work and those governing education (1977:184). The least that can be said is that a culture must always be transmitted, and work must always get done. In transmitting a culture to a new generation, a society commissions some to be the transmitters and others to be the acquirers, just as some are commissioned to produce and manage production while others are required to do what they are told and so to be mere reproducers. Those who make things are reproducers, in Bernstein's system, and not producers; only the latter are the innovators and inventors. The rules governing the workplace, like those governing the transmission and acquisition of culture in the classroom, are made by those who have the power to control what is made and what is learned. There will always be a hierarchy, but in the school and on the job that hierarchy may not always be visible. As there will always be a hierarchy, so there will always be rules governing the sequence in which things are made and lessons are learned. These rules, however, may often be implicit. If they are explicit in the classroom, the child knows what they are and can know in advance what is expected of students and how students will be judged. "However, where sequencing rules are implicit, only the transmitter knows them" (1977:18). Under these conditions, the rules consist of borrowings from various theories, but the student is operating in an environment that is essentially unknowable. Where rituals proceed according to sequences ordained by a secular clergy in education, or in work and politics, individuals can become habituated to being channeled while entertaining the illusion that they are freely charting their own course.

The cult of authority has some internal variations, even in a highly stratified society. Bernstein argues that, when rules for evaluating workers and students are relatively clear and more widely known, the *pace* at which work gets done on the job or in the classroom will be structured and predetermined. "Strong pacing, clear rules and standards, and a visible chain of command: these are the characteristics of schools and workplaces where 'sequencing' is highly developed" (Bernstein, 1977:117–18). In certain kinds of schools, however, and especially at certain ages, levels of development, and for certain classes, sequencing will be relatively vague. For the working class and for the youngest students, sequencing remains less developed than for those students entering the university or for students inured to the disciplines of relatively upper-class homes; at least that would appear to be the English case, according to Bernstein (1977:184–85). For the working class, their home and school training gives them little preparation to endure the strong and explicit rules that they will soon encounter at work, despite a general tendency for home and school to foreshadow the criteria of work for those from more elite backgrounds (ibid.:185).

In the United States, however, precisely the reverse may be the case, at least for more privileged students. As studies of the "young radicals" of the 1960s have made apparent, students who rebelled against the rules of a bureaucratically organized university may have been trained by their families to work according to rules that were far more implicit and relaxed with regard to pace and sequencing (Keniston, 1968). According to Keniston, students from the homes of the new middle-class or from the professions would have learned that their own values, integrity, and creativity should be taken as seriously as the requirements of a formal curriculum. Faced with the limited options and formal standards of the community, many dropped out while others rebelled. At the same time however, their fellow citizens in the working-classes in America may have been trained to color between the lines of boxes labeled pink, red, and blue in their school exercise books; these students would be less inclined to feel insulted at having to fill in the blanks and circles on grade sheets designed to code multiple choice examinations or at having to select from a limited array of options in the curriculum according to various disciplinary prerequisites. They were trained, at an early age, to stay the course.

Indeed, this contrast between the codes that mark the acquisition of culture in the relatively more or less advantaged classes in the United States and England is probably related to fundamental differences in the culture of the two countries, a point suggested, in fact, by Bernstein's insistence on an analogy between production and the transmission of culture. Those who produce will do so according to the basic codes of their society, whether those codes are highly formal or informal, explicit or implicit, clear and specific, or opaque and abstract, widely known or known only to the privileged who transmit and produce. Those who acquire and reproduce will simply provide a dim reflection of the dominant codes in their respective societies. I would suggest that the strong working-class emphasis in the United States on doing things in the right way at the right time, typified in the back-to-basics movements in religion, education, and politics, and personified in the presidency of Ronald Reagan, is a pale mirror image of the elitist standards to which the most professionalized and privileged classes adhere: the aping of those who produce by those who only reproduce, so do the young learn to revere their elders and the dead.

In a more traditional community, the individual is likely to be aware of the standards and constraints that bind individuals together; freedom operates within a visible framework and allows the individual the depths of private disagreement, and even heresy. In the modernized classroom, however, the reverse appears to be true; there are no apparent limits to discovery and production, while privacy is sacrificed to the scrutiny of the teacher whose judgments appear to penetrate the inner self of the pupil. In such an inauthentic surrounding, children learn that they are receiving two messages: one permission; the other filled with the vaguest of prohibitions. Children, therfore in a double bind, are likely to be criticized for not making full use of the opportunities available, and likely to be criticized if their notions of innovation fail to produce what the system expects. Later come the constraints of the larger society, whose messages about work and employment tend to place the individual in a similar double bind of responsibility for freely moving in directions that, in fact, are obligatory, predetermined, and yet unstated. Double binds have the effect of stifling initiative and raising anxiety; among children they may sometimes have more serious effects on the child's sanity (cf. Bateson et al., 1970).

Schools and churches have in common a tendency to appear more open than they are; corporations and medical institutions seem to have the opposite tendency. On the one hand, schools have diffuse standards for rewarding and promoting students and teachers, although those standards become increasingly specific as students and teachers become more advanced or specialized. Even at times of promotion to higher academic ranks, however, the ostensible standards are still quite vague; there are no clear indices for originality and creativity that inspire common agreement in academic departments; tenure is officially awarded on such abstract or diffuse grounds that it is difficult to command universal agreement or to mount an effective challenge to specific decisions. Covertly, however, more specific criteria may well be used to count the candidate's productivity, or nonacademic criteria of personal acceptability may be applied. While the rhetoric may remain academic and abstract, the underlying criteria that actually constrain such decisions and the actions of candidates may be nonacademic and concrete. This tendency to conceal and yet follow more quantifiable and limited criteria is one kind of inauthenticity found in the churches as well as the schools. Salvation is equally difficult to define in both systems, but the procedures for attaining its signs and rewards are far more specific, however covertly they may be followed in day-to-day practice. In practice and over the long haul, the successful institutionalization of the Protestant ethic often leads not to the spirit but to the letter of capitalism.

That generalization applies in capitalistic societies, of course, precisely because the boundaries of schools and churches are permeable to the effects of a capitalist economy. Autonomous in their appearance, schools and churches offer a latent, and perhaps sometimes unconscious, obedience to the authoritative requirements of a capitalist system that judges individuals and institutions by their fruits. Institutions may be no less prone to appear autonomous while still covertly obeying the wishes and standards of others.

The same tendency to submit to external authority leads, I have argued, to false claims of institutional autonomy and to an inauthentic application of institutional standards and authority in day-to-day decisions and practice. Herbert Read therefore advocates not a piecemeal approach to social change; the pressures from the larger society and the constraints of a capitalist economy will always frustrate the attempts to establish liberated zones in the family, the churches, or the schools. Perhaps it will not be too tedious to repeat here the quotation with which I began the first chapter: "A general spirit of revolt, such as I advocate here, is directed against the *totality* of an absurd civilization—against its ethos, its morality, its economy, and its political structure" (Read

1954:26; emphasis added). Such a revolt, of course, can be inspired and carried out only by a movement that establishes boundaries that cannot be penetrated by agents from the larger society or by the most persuasive of economic pressures to produce results for that society. Even small religious schools will need to prepare their students to pass tests devised in the bureaucracies of the state's educational establishments; and such schools will be under pressure to justify their independence by demonstrating to state examiners that they are producing citizens who can be "productive," i.e., hold jobs, make things, and staff offices. Only the strongest of boundaries maintained with proud autonomy can prevent such inauthenticity from corroding the most convinced and consecrated of local communities.

Of course, schools are only one kind of organization whose stated purposes are open but whose actions suggest a more limited and specific set of criteria for rewarding and promoting individuals through the grades or ranks. Churches may also claim to be open to diffuse aims, such as spiritual growth, but congregations that grow in numbers and in the size of their financial contributions may find that they receive far more attention and recognition, and exert more influence than other congregations, regardless of their spiritual achievements. On the other hand, it is widely known that business organizations may appear closed in their criteria for rewarding employees, but actually be open. For instance, executives who have lived up to the letter of the law, done their work, kept long hours, improved their skills, and enhanced the efficiency of their operations may find themselves passed by for promotion while others, more adept in the skills of personal influence within the organization, acquire higher office with relative ease, regardless of their devotion to duty or their productivity. The informal networks within an organization may make it possible for many individuals to acquire or wield extraordinary influence and power, although their formal qualifications may not be superior to those who are seldom consulted or incorporated into the making of important decisions for the organization. To meet the formal criteria for senior executive officer but to be excluded from the informal processes by which decisions are made is a source of profound personal anguish. Whenever there are two "systems" operating in any constitution or organization, one formal and the other informal, the informal system may be the one that carries the covert standards and criteria of the organization into action.

Autonomy, strong boundaries, and internal solidarity are the necessary, if not wholly sufficient conditions for authentic institutions. Read sums it up: "Such freedom, I argue, can only be preserved in small communities, free from a central and impersonal exercise of power, communities developing by mutual aid and with complete respect for the personality" (1954:25). Without those strong boundaries, even the most solidary and supportive of small communities will have to give covert recognition to the external pressures of the economy and the state.

As conflict becomes ritualized, organizations develop techniques for disguising their internal and external conflicts, and they develop explanations for problems that therefore appear intractable. That is why Kozol persistently attacks the noble sentiments of the well-to-do and the better educated for their sham. In his attack on American education, Kozol notes that school children in the suburbs are encouraged to enlarge their horizons and to become concerned about children in the inner cities, but that concern does not lead to a genuine enrichment of both groups or to enduring ties of affection and mutual responsibility. Visits are brief; even internships in inner city schools come to an end. The less privileged are left behind. Those who have studied the matter come to the conclusion that one individual can do nothing, and a few can do only a little more. A myth develops, which Kozol calls the myth of benign concern, benign, because the well-off are well intentioned but impotent; because all are trapped in a common fate, a social system that deprives its children of joy, regardless of race, creed, color, or national origin.

So long as conflict is ritualized, the drive to attain mastery and to exercise control can only have partial success and requires the acceptance of external constraints. Becker (1975) points out that a primitive technique for combining expanded social horizons with the drive for mastery is the moiety: the division of social life into "we" and "them", into two halves. As in any organized sport, there is a net or a line of scrimmage dividing those who are, in fact, seeking to come together. The line may be drawn between teams or neighborhoods, men and women, those who practice before the bar and those who have access to the bench. In any event, the division, into split halves enables congress to occur under set conditions. These are the rules of the game. The same organization also permits strivings for mastery and domination to come literally into play; there are winners and losers, and those who cross the line between teams or neighborhoods, villages or genders, must do so knowing that they are indeed in a contest for control. However, so long as conflict is ritualized, the rules for mastery are established not only by local custom but by the local authorities. Those who strive as they come together share a common fate in the sense that they are under the same rules and may suffer the same penalties for an infraction of those rules.

The external constraints imposed through the ritualization of conflict arouse the ire of the anarchist. Bakunin, as I have noted, was furious with Marx for insisting on playing the game according to the rules of democratic parliamentarism. The state, in setting the rules for class conflict, would ensure not only an unequal contest but the perpetuation of the state itself. In fact, democratic socialism could only enlarge the role of the state and expand its functions and domain over the class struggle. Marx's scenario of class conflict does remind us of the primitive organization of struggle into two opposed groups, but the scenario can only be played out under the aegis of the state. That was precisely Bakunin's objection to the Marxist programme for the Internationale: that mastery by the formal authority of the state could only become further institutionalized.

Modern social critics echo the anarchist's objection to formal authority. Let us return to Kozol's polemic against modern education. In one of his most telling passages, he complains that teachers encourage their students to engage in actions that promise mastery, real control over social events. These actions, however, always result in a perpetuation of specific contradictions. To perpetuate those contradictions is indeed the function of authority; it is the role of authority in fact to adjudicate the conflict between opposed forces in any society. (That, of course, was Becker's point about the primitive moiety.) For example, Kozol refers to the way teachers encourage students to do research on a social problem, write their representatives in congress urging public attention to the problem in question, and then wait for a reply. Under the aegis of the state, the reply is always appreciative of the student's work, encouraging of further effort, and promising. The promise is always the same; the state will receive these offerings of public interest and turn them to the public's benefit. What matters is not actual resolution of the conflict but a perpetuation of the exchange between those who rule and those who delegate to them authority over the public interest. The ritualization of social conflict always serves to strengthen the authority of those to whom the public interest is entrusted.

Coda

From the beginning of their discipline, sociologists have observed that social life requires a certain conspiracy to protect individuals from insults to their self-esteem and from personal injury. On one hand, normal social interaction is seen as a conspiracy even among unequals to preserve each others' "face" in social interaction, to permit an exchange that allows all parties to conceal the degree to which they suspect the others' motives and entertain doubts about the others' credibility. Without this façade, social interaction would not be smooth but full of unpleasant surprises; even a prison or a frankly exploitative relationship depends on a modicum of consent to keep up appearances. Sociologists therefore marvel not that there is so little smoothness in social life, but that there is so much. Social life is, in this view, an achievement of mutual conspirators who give a spurious or playful performance according to an agreed-upon script. A more polite way of stating it speaks of actors who have successfully institutionalized their beliefs and values in rules that govern everyday social life.

I have been arguing that the ritualization of social conflict enables a society to gain security and some continuity over time; discrepant ideas are rationalized, and discordant values given only a limited amount of toleration or free play in social life. On the whole, successful social systems become increasingly integrated on the basis of certain rules for ritualizing conflict. These rites acquire a certain moral justification; these are the rules that are always honored, if only in the breaches of social interaction. On the other hand, these breaches indicate an often widespread dissatisfaction about the rules and about those who manage to appear as if they play by those rules. In view of this latent conflict, social life appears to depend more on sham than on conspiracy. It is simply inauthentic.

To criticize inauthentic social systems, one needs a critical end point from which to look for what the surface of social life obscures, and it is to adopt such an end point that I have turned to some of the perspectives of anarchist thought. There is no doubt that these perspectives represent utopian aspirations for a secular religious community, aspirations that even few religious communities can satisfy. Take once more the notion of individuation as an example of how far this critical end point transcends specific social orders. Read argues that "The future unit is the individual, a world in himself, self-contained and self-creative, freely giving and freely receiving, but essentially a free spirit" (1954:39). The echoes here are plain enough; "freely have ye received . . . freely give." Anarchist thought, like early Christian preaching, presents a calling to become the first fruits of a new humanity above and beyond law and custom, state authority, or the tedium of normalcy.

The antinomian strains in Read's thoughts, like those of the New Testament, are nonetheless mingled with another strain that views the natural and social world as part of a larger order with its own laws. Read rejects the notion of the individual of the future as an egoist or superman; such figures, in any event, only invite others to submit themselves to the leader's arbitrary will as an escape from the anxieties of separate and free individuality. Instead, Read would have the individual fully aware of "the laws which govern his reactions to the group of which he is a member" (1954:40). These are not merely the local laws, to which the free individual owes no conscientious obedience, but the laws of reason. Among the latter are the rights to freedom and to equity, viz. the right to live under conditions that foster the full development of each person's capacities. To live to the fullest extent of one's own individuality, it is necessary, Read would argue, to free others from the constraints imposed by inequality. Otherwise, one lives at others' expense, and in so doing, diminishes one's own capacities.

There is no doubt that this critical vantage point requires an act of faith on the part of the sociologist. One has to leap beyond known tendencies and conditions to a standpoint that is beyond mere debunking and relativizing. The act of faith is that genuine freedom and equality are possible. Without such a vantage point for criticism, sociologists can only debunk without making any affirmations.

No doubt, some sociologists do merely hide their own utopian fantasies under the cloak of a severe and uncompromising criticism; all appears, then, as mere vanity to the sociological eye, that is, sets of illusions that allow individuals to believe that they have achieved more freedom and have more dignity than "the facts" would suggest. Such a debunking perspective typifies the work, for instance, of Erving Goffman, who spent a lifetime examining the collusion between individuals to maintain their respective illusions. The audience sustains the speaker's illusion, for instance, that the speaker is of absorbing interest, while the speaker allows the audience to believe that the speaker's remarks are spontaneous or at least prepared only for them (Goffman, 1981). In this way both sides of a verbal exchange collude to maintain their pride, to give the illusion of mutality and a meeting of minds, to allow one another to feel, if only for a moment, confirmed by the other's presence. It is a ritualistic technique of providing the illusion of spontaneous unity in a world where individuals know that they are alone, of perpetuating the lie rather than of recognizing it. Because the technique is only "half successful," like a ritual it must be repeated (O'Keefe, 1982:175). Because it is at least half successful, however, individuals who engage in these rituals of social interaction are persuaded that they may preserve the lie and, with it, perpetuate their despair and remorse over their self-deception.

In contrast to sociologists who, like Goffman, stress the symbiotic aspects of mutual deception, sociologists or theologians may stress the aggressive forms of social deception. One class persuades another to accept its values in order to deceive it concerning the true terms of its subordinate relationship. The rulers are said to rule by virtue of their virtues—a subterfuge that allows the dominated class to enjoy being dominated. Whether the parties to the relation are dominant or subordinate, sadistic or masochistic, the social contract maintains each party's pride. Religion itself can be a form of class domination, then, its missionary enterprise an "unbridled human self-assertion in religious disguise" (Niebuhr, 1953, 1:200). Even a Marxist ideology or a nation's civil religion, its belief that God has a mission in history for this nation in particular, is simply sinful pride. "The universalistic note in human knowledge becomes the basis of an imperial desire for domination over life which does not conform to it" (1953, 1:198).

In a society that is only partially secularized, it is only a "cultural fiction" that individuals are the source of a society's authority and that their well-being is the prime goal of the society itself. Social life is built on a collusion among individuals, between the leaders and their followers, between institutions and their clientele, to reinforce one another's narcissism. McDonald's, like other institutions, claims to make each customer number one. The electorate will accept their leader's illusions if the leaders will return the compliment to the followers; a great people deserves a great leader. To cement these ties and foster these illusions, the parties to the lie engage in certain rites that, like magical words, evoke each other's presence and create an imaginary fusion of the minds with common beliefs and shared values; however, the minds are still, in fact, quite separate, and each individual is, in the last analysis, no less vulnerable than before the ritualized exchange.

I have been arguing that to ritualize social conflict endangers the participants by giving them illusions of security that they can ill afford. To indulge a "false consciousness" about one's significance in any society is to entertain fanciful illusions that the leaders are not only powerful but caring, and these illusions of safety and of one's importance in the eyes of the powerful can be very danger-ous indeed. A social life based on lies can lead an entire commu-nity to the brink of self-destruction. The same lies therefore lead an entire society toward disaster. The more secular a society becomes, however, the fewer such illusions it sustains.

Without the shared lies of social life, individuals are left to their own devices to create techniques for feeling somewhat less help-less and more significant. That is, of course, what a neurosis attempts to do for the individual believer; it is a means of protect-ing the individual's sense of security and well-being, and prevent-ing further injury to the individual's wounded self. This is achieved at the cost of further isolation from others. In a wholly secularized society, one would necessarily look primarily to the individual's own delusions for the most chronic and widespread sources of false consciousness. As institutions and organizations become more prosaic and matter-of-fact in their objectives and less ritualized in their techniques for mobilizing their employees or constituents, the "magic" will increasingly go out of social life. Illusions of special power or importance will leave large-scale social units and find a home in the minds of individuals who are to that extent increasingly isolated from one another by their delu-sions. O'Keefe sums up the particular characteristics of modern societies in this way:

> Historically, magic has shrunk, falling back before the priests and then before the scientists. The implication is similar to the sugges-tion of Stanley Diamond: In complex civilizations in which man's symbolic powers are alienated, magic retreats, crippled, to its psy-chological base, and the obsessional-compulsive neurosis spreads rampantly (1982:275).

Weber put it more simply, in arguing that the spirit (pneuma, charisma) that animates social life with a particular enthusiasm and warmth has left modern institutions and survives, at the best, in small groups; there, individuals can still enjoy the temporary excitement of feeling at one with one another. Certainly their words have more profound effects on one another in small, face to face settings than in the programmed and formal speech of bureaucratic memoranda or in the set pieces of public speech. Even so, even in small groups, where what Goffman calls "face work" can more effectively preserve the participants from noticing or exposing each other's failings, the need for collusion persists and is perhaps even stronger than in the impersonal routines of office and agency. Whereas Durkheim was afraid that modern societies would reinforce their members' illusions about their own powers and importance and so attacked the ideology of individualism, Weber was more certain that an individual's illusions find little support in the continuous, specific, rule-governed routines of modern organizations. In a secular *society* there may be many illusions, but far fewer of them are collective and sustained.

Of the motives that kept *individuals* from freeing themselves from illusions concerning their own power and importance, the desire to feel the presence of a superior and life-giving force is no doubt the most prevalent and potent. It is to this striving for self-perpetuation that psychoanalysis attributes the magical and wishful thinking of the child, a thinking that persists under the apparently reasonable decisions of the adult. Agreeing with Otto Rank, Ernest Becker says that humans are "fate-creating agents" (1975:51). In abandoning equality in social fact, then, individuals recreate it in a sublime world where the inequalities are subsumed under a common, if not identical fate. What has been lost in solidarity is finally restored in the End that prevails over all separate and partial ends. A secular society does offer that single consolation, a common fate in death itself.

The tendency to build tabernacles, to sacralize a relationship, has its roots, of course, in the desire to transcend death. To make a relationship sacred is to engage in perhaps the most primitive form of accumulation: to preserve a relation by turning it into a thing that can be stored, protected, and preserved beyond the point of death. The attack on property, then, is simply a natural outcome of the process of secularization. Left to their own devices rather than to collective solutions to mortality, individuals will seek only that amount of mastery over the world and control over one another that is necessary for the survival of the system. The expansion of the realm of "freedom" over the sphere of "necessity" will intensify the desire to eradicate the past, to dispense with authority, to destroy rules, and to turn the process of acquiring mastery into a form of play. In a secular society, it will be unnecessary to sacralize the temporary relations of domination that are useful for accomplishing a specific task or the inevitable result of forms of social play.

Even in a secular society the individual understands that we owe our origin to a society and to a civilization that have given us birth, life, an identity, and a way of life. The individual also assumes on the other hand, that each of us has an uncommon fate. To stifle awareness of our origins and obligations is to lose half of the truth; piety, whether it focusses our obligations on the church, the nation, the state, or on a distant providence reminds us of that part of the truth. Never to know how unique and unrepeatable each person is, however, is to lose sight of one's sole destiny or vocation, to use a traditionally religious term for this experience. The great temptation is to exalt one half of the truth over the other, to become dutiful in the extreme but exceedingly normal, or to become, on the other hand, a character that is less individuated than idiosyncratic or narcissistic. The pathology of a society depends on which part of the truth it owns at the expense of the other.

Individuation in a secular society requires imagination, strength, vitality, and the ability to empathize or sympathize with others in their joy and pain, to render aid and to rescue where such help is needed; to cooperate and invest in strategies for getting work done and goods distributed; to make plans with others and to carry them out simply, swiftly, and with a minimum of pain and confusion. While Kropotkin exalted the capacities of primitives, savages, barbarians, and citizens of the medieval city for rendering mutual aid, he notes that a savage who has offended custom or injured a clan member is liable to various forms of punishment and may well lose the will to live (1904:112). Solidarity without the full development of the self has severe drawbacks. Kropotkin also notes how many of his fellow prisoners, in the dungeons of St. Petersburgh, lost, like the most primitive savage, their own will to live. Many sickened and died, while others took their own lives (1962:246). The will to live fully and freely is essential to healthy individuation in any society.

In the anarchist perspective, I find a critical point of view that looks on a society as though it were a secular religious community, a lay church, in which the spirit moves freely and yet builds up social order, and in which whatever builds up the community liberates the individual. Theirs is not merely a romantic view of society, in which the best society is least developed; no anarchist would argue that the individual is a free spirit engaged in a life and death struggle with crushing institutions; on the contrary, no individual can be fully free without a society that is itself fully alive, full of variety, and perhaps full of conflict. At the same time, the critical end point is not simply a restatement of a "classical" view in which individuals simply embellish, encapsulate, embroider, and otherwise adorn a social structure in the way that a Corinthian capital completes the column on which it rests. On the contrary, the critical end point envisages a society that is no freer than the most constrained individual, and in which the consummation of individual lives constitutes the fulfillment of the social order itself. There is no doubt that the anarchic dream draws heavily on sectarian Christian religion and holds out a secular, millenial hope.

The anarchist view is attractive primarily because it embraces (rather than conceals) the paradox in the relation of the individual to the community. That paradox is a familiar one: while individuals are who they are by virtue of their social origins and their social context, to become an individual is to become more fully a self that is unique, unrepeatable, and singular, although not incomprehensible or incomparable, or alone. The paradox is sometimes expressed in theological terms as the relation between divine providence and divine election; the same destiny provides for all and yet leads each down a separate path. The theological terms may seek to entertain the paradox in a single, exemplary person; one who is both fully human and fully divine; a model for all and yet one of a kind; the first fruit of many brethren and yet one who has been all the brethren may yet become; one who has done all that is needed for salvation, and yet one who requires that each person work out his or her salvation in fear and trembling. The paradox has many theological forms and is familiar enough without elaboration. The point is simply that anarchism embodies not a contradictory but a paradoxical view of the primary relation of self to society. The two presuppose and require each other, and yet each provides the conditions for the other's existence and development. It is a paradox that makes sense only to the individual who, over a lifetime, becomes increasingly aware of his or her social roots while pursuing a selfhood that cannot be reduced to or predicted from his or her origins: a selfhood that is essential and yet always partly a mystery until the very end.

Despite the repetition, I wish to quote again certain key passages in Read's writing. At times he speaks of the individual's awareness of "the laws which govern his reactions to the group of which he is a member" (1954:40); he also speaks of reason, of natural law, of the general principles of solidarity with the human community, or of equity (cf. 1954:41, 107, 155). But there is something aesthetic in this notion of the individual, in a harmony of opposites, the one tending toward universality and the other toward uniqueness. After all, Read was a critic and historian of art. Read's notion of the individual combines transcendence and immanence, self-regard and regard for others. There is something mythic about this notion of the individual, and indeed, Read notes that, for the anarchist, the complete individual is of heroic proportions. Like the mythic hero who slays the demon—a representative of the father—the anarchist "comes of age; he disowns the father; he lives in accordance with his own ego-ideal. He becomes conscious of his own individuality" (1954:97). Unlike the fascist hero or genius, however, the anarchist is fully aware of the extent to which all humans are bound to one another rather than separated into groups and is unlikely ever again to surrender individuality either to a group or to a heroic leader.

In an inauthentic society, of course, it is extremely difficult to be aware of one's uniqueness or solidarity with others. One's uniqueness is a private affair; there is no ground on the basis of which to make comparisons, so solitary is one's experience and incomparable one's situation. One's universality is not based on any natural law or any obligation to the human community. To begin with, the underlying structure or framework within which one's development is first measured is the property of a professional monopoly that owns and controls the symbols of human development; on the other hand, such measures remain covert. One knows that one falls short of the ideal, but like Kafka's hero in *The Trial*, one never meets the source of one's sense of guilt and never comes to trial; the judge never appears and the criteria on the basis of which one stands accused never becomes clear or specific. Nonetheless, one knows that these criteria are there, especially in an inauthentic system that reassures one that one is free. A framework that is covert can be a source of considerable anguish.

Conclusion

Of course, it is very easy, while exploring the contradictions in a society, to fall into contradictions in one's own thinking. Certainly, anarchism is not a seamless web of thought free from all contradictions. There is no lack of commentary, however, on these "paradoxes" in anarchist thought, and I need not repeat them here. Instead, I wish to point out what makes these contradictions intelligible and necessary as part of the anarchist program for the liberation of social systems from "social tyranny" as Kropotkin put it: the tyranny of habit, unreflective thinking and of moral reflexes. The goals of the anarchist, like Freud's goals for psychoanalysis, are, in fact, revolutionary: the constitution of a new order literally unlike any previous formation of either custom or character. Their projects require the removal of what Freud and the anarchists both called repression. Without the cult of authority, what appears to be an idealistic program becomes a realistic appraisal of what individuals can do to unite and act together in ways that enhance rather than constrict the range of free association.

In this chapter, I have focussed primarily on educators and intellectuals, but the analysis of moral teaching as a form of tyranny can extend to science. If ever there were a cult of authority in modern societies, it is found in the respect given to those who probe the mysteries of living things, of materials, of the planet, and of the universe. If indeed anarchists are dreamers, their program to rid themselves of the authority of science would be clearly utopian; listen, however, to Bakunin:

> While rejecting the absolute, universal and infallible authority of men of science, we willingly accept the respectable, although relative, temporary, and restricted authority of scientific specialists, asking nothing better than to consult them by turns, and be grateful for their precious information as long as they are willing to learn from us in their turn (1972:230).

The problem is that science, to borrow Kropotkin's term, becomes an "institution," a set of relationships that puts distance between ordinary people and scientists, and perpetuates an extension of the scientists' authority over everyday life. The anarchists' own strategy (as of psychoanalysis) is to relate instruction of various sorts, the implicit codes by which people live and their explicit reasons for living that way, to the "facts and events of everyday life" (Kropotkin). The method is part and parcel of the cure. As science becomes part of "the immediate and real life of each individual," it will be far more useful and far less pedantic and doctrinaire (Bakunin, 1972:233). Of course, that happy relation of method to outcome, of social analysis to the formation of a new, flexible, and reciprocal relationship between people and scientists, cannot occur overnight. In the meantime, before the revolution and under the continuing conditions of repression by scientific, religious, and political institutions, scientists will still have a contribution to make, but their contribution can only be theoretical, abstract, and pertinent not to everyday life but to the general conditions under which people live (ibid., p. 232). That is, science as we know it, given to statistical inference, and therefore unable to know whether a particular individual should or should not act upon its findings, is simply unable to give any but the most abstract and hypothetical advice about the conditions and probabilities under which something might happen. It remains to individuals to make up their minds and take their risks accordingly.

Under conditions in which scientists work more closely to the facts of everyday life, however, they will be able to speak the truth to an individual and be fully conversant with the many aspects of that person's life: emotions, relationships, working conditions, anxieties, hopes and fears, and all the other factors that operate in that person's life. Only so can science contribute to the liberation and full development of each individual that is the goal both of psychoanalysis and of the anarchist program. Until solidarity and equality obtain, however, science will remain an institution that acts at a considerable distance from those whom it habitually affects. The laboratory of the nuclear physicist and of the weapons specialist is no doubt a case in point.

Under the conditions of repression that now obtain wherever there is a state and wherever there are institutions, the natural tendency of individuals to unite together in new forms of communities still is alive, but it is not well. The ritualization of conflict introduces a pathological expression of that tendency to unite, so that individuals become passive rather than active in their relationships, habitual rather than spontaneous, and prone to taking the moral authority of their institutions for granted. They live in a world in which moral advice is given with the preface that "studies have shown" or "7 our of 10 doctors recommend." It is a world in which we are all categorized, and it is as burdensome for the scientists as it is for those whom they "serve." Placed at a considerable remove from the everyday lives of their patients, for instance, doctors are loath to make decisions regarding the cessation of feeding or other functions for the incurably or terminally ill; they must leave such decisions to the friends and families, not to the patients themselves, who may be equally unwilling to make poignant and painful decisions, while their scientific advisors must remain in the realm of the hypothetical and can speak only of general conditions and probabilities. The human community that might unite doctors and citizens in a community of shared responsibility and common action becomes a place where each party must hedge bets, pay malpractice insurance, and feel irresponsible, or guilty. With less authority, the institution that we call medicine might be less defensive and more helpful; those who pay the bills might be better served and less impoverished. Under the conditions of solidarity and equality, new forms of common action unite those who suffer and those who care for them in a more truly humane community. It really is as simple as that.

5 Rituals in a Secularizing Society: The Precarious Condition of the Cult of Authority

In the preceding chapters, I have considered some of the ways that the state, as a framework that limits the imagination, insinuates itself into the consciousness of the individual and becomes a source of punishment or reprisal that inhibits the spirit of revolt. Ritualistic social interaction, I have argued, reinforces that framework and further intimidates the rebellious spirit. Certainly collective ceremonies may dramatize the power of the state, manufacture its legitimacy, and mobilize support and praise, even more than do the ritualized patterns of social life I have so far considered. The rites of military display dramatize the state's power, and memorial services for those who died in the service of the state provide subtle reminders of the power of the state over both life and death. The same rites of display or commemoration may also manufacture a certain legitmacy for the state; no one who dies in the state's service dies in vain, or without a certain glory. During political campaigns, of course, candidates for office seek to associate themselves with the symbols of power and authority: witness the American election campaigns in which candidates review troops or have themselves pictured with planes, ships, and guns. Candidates also campaign for office by paying honor to the dead: witness the timely and highly controversial visit of Helmut Kohl and Ronald Reagan to Bitburg cemetary in the days preceding an important regional election in West Germany in 1985. The controversy itself indicates a widespread cynicism about the political use of collective memories and symbols for private gain; the same cynicism typifies the antiritualist notions of anarchist thinkers. Here, I intend to examine the case

136

for the most formal and splendid ceremonies and to ask whether, under certain circumstances, ritual can serve the purpose of social transformation even in modern societies.

There is no doubt, as Becker reminds us, that societies have always tried to achieve "a unification of experience, a simplification of it, and a rooting of it in a secure source of power" (1975:68). What distinguishes modern societies from earlier ones is not only the amount of complexity to be simplified, and the corresponding demand for an institution like the state that could provide at least the appearance of unity to social life, but the difficulty of imagining precisely the cultural sources of unity and simplicity. In societies dominated by authorities that were as sacred as they were secular, one could at least imagine that there were, in the body of the king, in the edicts of the courts, in the jurisdictions of the magistrates, a unity that transcended all divisions, and a will that could bring complexity into some sort of order. That capacity to imagine was heightened, no doubt, by solemn occasions, rituals of inauguration and enthronement, processions and other displays of the power of the state; the appearance of unity was strengthened by forms of deference in social life that united the ordinary household with the household of the king or emperor.

These sources of the historical imagination have not entirely disappeared. In the rites of Nazi enthusiasts or of the Soviet State, we have recent examples of attempts to unify complex societies by capturing the hearts and imaginations of the citizenry. I shall return to these rituals later in this chapter. The sacred, which provided simplicity and unity to social life by rooting the populace "in a secure source of power," has enjoyed only intermittent and tragic successes in modern nation-states: tragic, because these successes have involved masses of individuals in a common fate that few desired and virtually no one could entirely avoid or control.

There is a certain "as if" quality to all ritualized social encounters, an element of make believe. Much depends, however, on how compartmentalized from the ordinary world such ritualized actions may be. The more sharply rituals are demarcated from everyday life the more readily individuals can lend themselves to ritual and take their parts without being distracted by complexity or deceived by their performances. Once ritual prescribes actions that have become truly spontaneous through long use and familiarity, individuals are *least* likely to feel that they are merely engaging in culturally prescribed motions, fulfilling a traditional role, or confused about where the outside world begins and their own selves end. Sharply defined rites offer a world of strong individuality as well as profound sharing. Here, then, I will explore the limitations to the anti ritualist biases in anarchist and psychoanalytic thought.

To begin with, I will argue that ritual, narrowly conceived, may serve some of the purposes that anarchists hold most dear. By "narrowly conceived," I mean to refer to rituals that are sharply distinguished from various ceremonies, rallies, spectacles, and other less durable, less formal, and less distinctive forms of collective renewal. I wish to separate rituals per se from the forms of social life that are ritualistic in one way or another. My point is simply that merely ritualistic forms of healing or instruction, of politics or of administration, can only ape the manners but not perform the functions of *ritual*. There are, I will argue, several conditions under which ritual, as distinct from ceremonies or merely formal social routines, may be liberating and creative; some of these conditions are social, while others are psychological.

The point is that collective ceremonies become "mere" formalities when improperly and only vaguely framed in various rites; that is why national ritual often makes public solemnity seem unconvincing and contrived. It may well be that the symbols of the nation only acquire the force of moral authority in more local and explicitly sacred usage during rites that are more distinctly set apart from mundane of practical activities. There, at the local level, the symbols of the nation may still command a certain allegiance, where memorial services gather the faithful and the pledge of allegiance in the local classroom is a rite that can be slighted only at some peril to the individual. The same symbols, coopted by the state for its purposes, may command less assent and inspire far less conviction, the more manipulative and strategic their use becomes in the effort to mobilize support and to manufacture legitimacy for specific candidates and parties.

Certainly the American state has borrowed heavily from the piety and imagination that come to play in ritual. Take, for example, the millenarian aspects of political ideology in the United States. John Wilson notes that:

> The crusading impulse in American society, which has been prone repeatedly to identify one *final* evil to be eradicated or one *last*

wrong to be righted, also embodies millenarian elements. The pattern originated in evangelical circles of the early nineteenth century in specific social reform movements. By the twentieth century, however, the form of the crusading appeal was deeply suffused through American political life. So the nation could have its entry into a world war plausibly explained as a "war to make the world safe for democracy." Equally plausible was the subsequent crusade against a great alternative world order, atheistic communism (1979:106).

In borrowing so heavily from religious enthusiasm, however, the nation has taken that impulse from the context of religious celebration and transposed it to the context of the state. Within the context of a religious revival, the resolution to transform the world once and for all through one final effort subordinates reason to faith, and properly so; the goal transcends any neat calculation of means and ends. In the hands of the state, however, the same combination of religious enthusiasm and reason subordinates the former to the latter; the pious impulse to transform the world serves the ends of the state to remove its major competitors from the international field. A war-to-end-all-wars is, of course, a war that leaves one state without serious rivals. Outside the context of religious celebration, the pious hope for Zion becomes a nationalistic Zionism, and popular hopes and loyalties become closely associated with the state and its own goals and interests.

The same observation can be made of the strain toward purity in American religious and political movements. Released from the context of ritual, the spirit becomes puritanical. In John Wilson's (1979:104) view, puritanism is a strong motif in American culture that has made all those who espouse it dissatisfied with "the world." Usually, the dissatisfaction is directed at others, immigrants or other deviants, whose behavior differs from the standards of a particular group. Often, the identity, survival, and mobility of a group depends on strong, puritanical discipline (the ascetic discipline of Black Muslims comes to mind). Whether it is an ethnic group, or a generation seeking to perpetuate itself or gain control over others, matters less than Wilson's primary generalization about Puritanism, i.e., that it has a wide variety of sources and expressions in American culture and enjoys temporary revivals among those groups primarily disconcerted by social change. Puritanism also can find aid and comfort in a millenarianism that adopts change for the sake of ending all change and to

initiate a prolonged period of harmony and stability. In the hands
of the state, of course, puritanism becomes less obsessive concerning certain minutiae of good behavior and more disposed, as
Wilson reminds us, to dissociate "us" from "them" and to separate the good from the evil (1979:103). Certainly, self-righteous-
ness in American politics and foreign policy is nothing new; in
recent years, American presidents have been more explicit in their
denunciation of various enemies' disregard for human rights or
democratic institutions, and the separation of the world between
Americans and the "evil empire" of the East has become more
acute.

Rituals, like the Puritan aspect of American culture, often have
been able to provide the sharp boundaries between a world
purified of all contamination and an environment fraught with
danger. In the framework of a sharply demarcated rite, evil
thoughts and spirits, along with pollutants of other sorts, are
systematically purged from the body of the faithful. The attempt
to actually purge the extraneous or the contaminating influences
from the body of the faithful outside such a ceremonial context is
an indication of the failure of certain rites to guarantee purity;
witness the Inquisition in the wake of the Reformation's attack on
Catholic ritual. The same insistence on ridding the body politic of
pernicious influences, however, may indicate that the state has
borrowed from the context of religious ceremony; the enthusiasm
for purity, once it breaks through the context of local rite and
communal revival, can lead to efforts to purge the nation of all
those who are reactionary, revisionist, or racially impure. The
genie, once let out of the bottle of ritual, has a life of its own and
will serve any master on the left or on the right.

As Freud pointed out, ceremonies represent "the sum of all the
conditions under which something not yet absolutely forbidden
becomes permissible" (1907; 1963:23). Ritual therefore requires
individuals to act "as if" some action may become possible so that,
at some time or place, it may yet *be* possible. It is this "as if"
quality of ritual that arouses the antagonism of the critic who
wishes to see more concrete and effective social action in the
immediate present. On the other hand, it is the same capacity of
ritual to point beyond the realm of what is now feasible or real that
gives to ritual its potential for liberation. The controversy among
critics of ritual is due in part, then, to the very ambiguity of ritual
itself. I will take up the controversy in more detail later in this
chapter.

The Shape of Ritual

Rituals vary in two major respects that account for some of their capacity to transform a social context and offer the prospect of liberation. One of these characteristics concerns the relation of any ritual to what becomes the outside world: the world of nonbelievers, of nonparticipants, and of the profane or unworthy. Some rituals establish a clear and firm line separating the world of faith from everyday reality and the inside from the outside; other rituals are more open to intrusions and other influences from the mundane world. Another characteristic that varies from one ritual to another (or even in the same rite over time) is the degree to which the shape of the ritual itself dictates what is actually said or done within the ceremony. The more participants are free to choose what they say or do, the more the ritual will seem like "mere ceremonial." Variations in these two characteristics suggest why some rituals offer genuine possibilities of liberation and transformation, while others seem like "mere ceremonial."

These two factors are not those most frequently used in what is a growing sociological literature of rituals. Mary Douglas (1970) identifies "grid" and "group" as two aspects of rituals that are extremely important for understanding processes of social control. The "group" aspect of a ritual provides for more or less solidarity among members; the more "group," the more a society requires its members to act out in various ways the standards of that group. Through ritual, communities achieve an identity that separates members from outsiders who do not know how to eat, dress, or talk properly (and whose ideas or values are therefore correspondingly suspect). The "grid" aspect of a ritual models the hierarchy in any society: the bishops, priests, and deacons; the presidents, vice-presidents, managers, and workers; those who labor with symbols, and those who work with things. The more complex the hierarchy in a society, the more shades of deference come into play within the content of the ritual. For Mary Douglas (1970), there is a fearful symmetry between the body politic and the individual's body, a symmetry framed in ritual so exactly that the ritual carries forward everyday life into solemn occasions with relatively little disruption and discontinuity. When ritual models and enshrines a social order, there is little room for the play of myth, hope, and fantasy; options, whether few or many, reflect the range of choices and the degree of complexity in the larger society.

Perhaps the most complete sociological account of the way rituals work in modern societies is in Randall Collins's excellent *Conflict Sociology*. There, Collins (1975:166ff.) distinguishes two dimensions, authority and social density, which appear to anticipate Douglas's grid and group, respectively. As Collins notes, "a multifactor theory is more useful as a calculating device than as a typology-producing machine," but his factors do produce an interesting and useful typology along these two dimensions (1982:166). Logically enough, in a society where social density is "high," there are strong pressures toward conformity, high degrees of "surveillance" and isolation from outside social contacts. In a society where authority is "high," there are many shades of status or power and relatively extreme differences between the individuals of highest and lowest degree. Where both density and authority are "high," therefore, the burden on rituals to communicate and control is exceptionally heavy. The more people interact, Collins argues, the more their common life demands expression, creates a common focus, and arouses strong feelings; no wonder that ritual carries much of the burden of sustaining social life under these conditions. The same considerations apply to ways in which a society maintains proper patterns of deference between unequals.

Especially in modern societies, however, it is is necessary to ask whether rituals mirror or distort their social surroundings. Both Collins and Douglas operate under the assumption that rituals will somehow reflect the surrounding society. For example, where boundaries between Catholics and Protestants or between Christians and Jews are strong, ritual will dramatize the boundaries between the faithful and those outside. Again, where a society has a relatively elaborate and rigorous hierarchy of status or power, a ritual will provide an equally impressive display of different degrees of authority. If there has been a change in modern societies in the relation between rituals and their social context, however, the possibilities are far more complex. Rituals, indeed, may dramatize boundaries where none need exist. If, in the modern city, individuals have many partial and transient contacts with individuals from other racial, religious or ethnic communities, the rites that formerly cemented and dramatized such differences may provide images of cohesion that are not only lost, but no longer necessary. On the other hand, the rituals may hold out the image of a cohesion that, although currently lost, is still longed-for; no longer necessary for the social system, such cohesion may still seem desirable and, in the context of the rite itself, still possible.

In the same way, rituals that provided a model for relatively simple differences in status may seem outmoded and unnecessary in a world where the division of labor and the organization of bureaucracies make such differences exceedingly complex and difficult to grasp. The same rituals, however, may suggest that a simpler and more responsive hierarchy might well be possible in a world that has become far too complicated. Such rituals, then, could hold out the hope and the possibility of a social transformation. It is possible, for instance, that traditional rites have lagged so far behind the development of modern societies that they do hold out the image of a radically different social order, one that is far more solidary and equalitarian, more responsive and trustworthy, than one can find in an industrial and bureaucratized society. Newer rites may offer more limited hopes for transformation, since their form too closely resembles the complexity and vague organizational boundaries of the modern world. They are more useful as ways to mobilize popular support and manufacture legitimacy for those who conduct them.

If a ritual fails to provide a clear and distinct frame that separates the rite from everyday life, certainly that ritual will not have the same long-term consequences as it does when it provides a dramatic and contrasting episode outside the normal course of social life. How will a state of affairs be announced, e.g., a succession or the end of rivalry, a death or a new age, when ritual simply provides a ceremonial aura for activities that are largely routine? Again, if ritual fails to prescribe most of its contents, it will not have the same long-term consequences as a ritual that, in fact, makes every sequence, every exchange, every contribution and response obligatory and essential to the completion of the rite. How will ritual that allows for many options and variations from one performance to the next convey to individuals that their actions are complete and irrevocable?

Rituals that fail to integrate form with content may provide a model for social life in which individuals can improvise without immediate correction and reinterpret their obligations without chastisement. Authority and loyalty never come to the crucial test. In suggesting that some rituals provide distinctive frames and highly specific contents, while others negotiate the relation of form to content, I hope to indicate a range of possible consequences for the larger society, consequences that do not fit Collins's notion of religion as making the ultimate appeals for "moral solidarity" and "obedience." Under certain conditions, ritual may simply leave appeals for loyalty and solidarity to other institutions, to the media, perhaps, or to the central agencies of the state. Where the media fail to enlist loyalties, the authorities may have to do the persuading. It is no wonder either that the conventions of major parties during an American presidential campaign should so resemble religious revivals or that politicians should demand control over—and continuous attention from—the mass media. When other rituals fail, these institutions must provide the basis for cohesion.

Distinguishing Ritual from Ritualized Action

Rituals are artificial frameworks—artifacts of social interaction. For a particular time, individuals who may know each other in other contexts agree on a temporary framework for coming together and talking about whatever unites or divides them. Of course, any formality does the same thing; it provides a circumstance within which specific subjects are raised and others are safely ignored. But ritual specifies the kind of discourse and other exchanges that will take place.

Rituals vary in how closely they specify the content of what will be exchanged. In some rituals, topics for discussion are never really problematical. In the ritual of the courtroom, however, the judge must decide whether a specific line of questioning or an exhibit is relevant to the case in hand. In the course of a wedding or a funeral, the content of the ritual is more clearly specified in advance; one does not eulogize at a wedding or make promises at a funeral. Some rituals specify who will speak on various topics; judges reprimand and sentence; lawyers interrogate and object. Brides and bridegrooms make promises; the clergy interrogate or pronounce. Again, rituals specify the sequence of speakers: first the clergy, then the laity; first the lawyer for the prosecution, then the lawyer for the defense. Any form that specifies the order in which specific individuals will take their roles and speak on specific topics has gone a long way to determining the content of what is said and done. Narrative or gossip, on the other hand, always threatens formalities since their content is extemporaneous and spontaneous, the very opposite of a ritualistic activity.

The participants in rituals are sometimes carried away, literally transported, during the course of the rite; sometimes participation simply requires a particular type of conduct. The range of variation among rituals in this respect reflects the degree to which rituals provide a frame that is sharply opposed to the framework of everyday life. In the most feverish revivals or tribal orgies, a few individuals stay sober precisely so that they can come to the rescue of those who are slain by the spirit or transported with ecstasy; the task of the sober ones is to carry out those who have collapsed and to resuscitate them so that the ritual can be carried on to its proper conclusion. In other rites, notably those of secular trials of various sorts, the focus is on disciplined deportment; there, only one or two referees or marshalls may be sufficient to come to the rescue or to punish those who are carried away during the proceedings. The critical difference between a religious revival, and a courtroom is that the former differs more sharply from everyday life.

That difference in the way rituals are framed makes it possible for a revival to transform everyday life, if only momentarily, whereas a judicial trial or teaching in a classroom solemnizes the prevailing authorities. Compared with the most sharply framed ritual, however, a revival is more like a carnival where individuals make believe and take on more clearly contrived roles than those ordained by a rite whose frame is solid and distinct. On the other hand, they (revivals) are more distinct from everyday life than other rites, for example, trials requiring tests of intellectual or physical strength. A less complete suspension of everyday reality occurs in the courtroom or the concert hall; even there, however, any intrusions from the outside are prevented or swiftly punished lest the frame of the secular ritual be broken. In fact, the intrusion of the outside world into a lecture hall has been criticized by Goffman (1981) as upsetting the ritual of formal communication, just as Lasch (1969) has criticized the intrusion of spectators into the game, or of audiences into the play. Imagine, then, a continuum, from the most to the least sharply framed of rites, where at one end everyday life is transcended, and at the other end the authorities that govern everyday life come temporarily into view and receive their due.

The discussion in this book so far has concerned the ritualization of everyday life in the schools or at work, in neighborhoods, occasionally in politics and the offices of the state. There, conflict between people and the authorities, between generations, or between social classes is ritualized in a way that makes that conflict both more enduring and less intense, more symbolic and less direct. The parties to the conflict take on roles that dignify the authority of the system in question and confer a limited status on the individual as a representative of one category or another. These are the rituals that make normalcy oppressive and resemble more precisely the patterns of everyday life. There, the voice of reason coincides with the voice of authority. In that respect, the priestly paradigm that I described in the Introduction is correct. The prophetic paradigm, however, suggest that the rites of the courtroom or classroom, lecture hall or assembly are partial, incomplete, in competition with one another. The rites of the secularized world offer little contrast with everyday life because their forms are compatible with a variety of contents; consequently, they are easily interrupted and offer no final word on various subjects.

As in the courtroom, it is entirely likely that the procedures followed in clinical or professionalized settings also belong in this category of less authoritative and more highly vulnerable rituals. A number of writers frequently argue, in fact, that the professions have aped the controls and manners of the priests in order to more fully impress and dominate their clients and patients; the criticisms note, however, that these professional ceremonies fail adequately to separate the sacred from the mundane or to make certain procedures seem to be wholly obligatory. There are too many gaps and too much resemblance to the mundane world to command assent and disarm disbelief. What makes these rituals incomplete and vulnerable can also be seen in religious rites that increasingly employ modernized or everyday language, display ordinary moods and distinctly active or passive voices, and leave many arrangements to the options of those who perform and participate in them. To the extent that they also fit this picture, even ecclesiastical rites fail to offer a final and lasting sentence. That tendency, I would argue, can be observed across a wide range of religious settings, from evangelical television to the modernized ceremonies of even very traditional churches. The prophetic paradigm suggests, then, that rites in a secular society make the cult of authority itself temporary and unconvincing.

Comparisons are always difficult, of course, but one recent work on the rites of nations makes it easier for us to illustrate the precarious condition of the cult of authority in secularizing societies. In her recent book on *The Rites of Rulers,* Christel Lane (1981) compares the rites of the so called "civil religion" in America with the rites of Soviet Russia and of Nazi Germany. Although she does not consider a typology of the sort I am offering, her description points toward three of the four types in this proposed schema; the Nazi ceremonies, the Soviet, and the American.

It would appear that Nazi rituals were far more dramatic, further set apart from ordinary life, and therefore more sharply framed than Soviet rites. (See 2 and 3 in table 1.) On the two countries' use of fire and light as symbols, Lane notes, "Soviet ritual specialists stress the secular meaning of this group of symbols, while National Socialists emphasized its pagan origins and associations" (1981). Hitler's "blood flag," for example, was used to "consecrate" other flags by establishing and conveying "irrational, mystical" connections, hardly the mundane notions associated with the Soviets' use of the red flag to connote socialism per se (ibid.). The Soviets, like the Nazis, employed massive demonstrations and spectacles, but there is something clearly extraordinary in the Nazi case, an aura that suggests the presence of a frame sharply defining the sacred elements of the ceremonies apart from mundane meanings.

Soviet rites, on the other hand, were apparently far more orderly, constrained, and carefully sequenced than the Nazi spectaculars. The "confusion, illogicality and anti-rationality" of the Nazi rites embody "the degenerate and confused myth-like notions" of Nazi ideology; by way of contrast, Soviet rites were "very restrained" and allowed for little in the way of appeal to "physical urges and base instincts" (Lane 1981). In a society based on highly rational forms of social organization, the Nazi rituals could have had a transformative influence; they might have been "morphogenic" rather than morphostatic in function (cf. D'Aquili, et al., 1979:253).

In the Nazi case (see table 1), the form of the rituals hardly specified its content; masses of people waving red flags in Russia would mean something quite different. Lane makes that quite clear. The form could as easily have specified a different sequence of gestures, a different set of colors, and a variety of proceedings, whereas, in other rites, confession must always proceed absolution, petition and thanksgiving always precede consecration. The Nazi torch and flag only made sense when spelled out in racial myth and national prophecy, in party dogma or national policy. I would argue, in fact, that the Nazi rituals failed rather than succeeded. Indeed, these temporary fascist ecstasies failed to drain revenge and hatred from the body politic or to point effectively to consummations in another era. It was arguably the failure of ritual that left the slow work of extermination to the state. By the same argument one can say that it is the failure of the contrived rituals of the Soviet state that makes the police system and the mental hospitals such necessary items in the repertoire of the Soviets.

Arguments about ritual need, therefore, to be stood on their head, literally inverted, when one discusses modern rather than simpler social systems. In the simplest of societies, rituals express passions that cannot elsewhere find satisfaction in everyday life and demands for satisfaction that are not totally prohibited. In complex societies, however, political rituals do not insulate these strivings from everyday life and make these strivings available for others to mobilize through party machinery and military conscription.

Of course, the United States also enjoys political rituals whose form does not wholly specify or require a certain content and whose frame does not sharply distinguish the ceremony from the mundane (see table 1, no. 4). Lane describes the rites of the American political system in terms that distinguish them both from Nazi and Soviet ceremonials. Detailed comparisons would take too much space, but it should be enough to suggest that Lane (1981) finds American rites such as Thanksgiving Day or Memorial Day entirely compatible both with conventional religion and conventional morality. In a class with other national holidays commemorating various presidents or the birth of the nation, these rites confirm ordinary practices and values while leaving the individual considerable room to maneuver in private life. The same rites, I would argue, do not require a specific content or have a form that is indistinguishable from the content.

Precisely because the rites affirming American national identity are so secular, they will fail to contain and satisfy a wide range of passions for domination or revenge, for victory or for vainglory; these passions will necessarily find outlets in other forms of activity, whether in sports or politics, adventurism or military aggression. As recent events in India will attest, when temples are destroyed, individuals and groups may well seek more immediate and less symbolic forms of satisfaction. The failure of American rites to dramatize and effect the symbolic renewal of the nation, to posit a new future purified of old passions, and to bind individuals into a common destiny, will make the achievement of mutual responsibility and a coherent national policy through political action both more critical and more problematical. The burden on the political process may, in fact, exceed the ability even of a political campaign filled with moral enthusiasm to mobilize and contain the worst as well as the best of human strivings.

Table 1: Types of Rituals

Relation of Form to Content	Boundary with Everyday Life	
	Distinct	Indistinct
High Specificity	1	2
Low Specificity	3	4

1. Ideal-typical religious ritual
2. Soviet civic rituals
3. Nazi ceremonies and spectacles
4. American civil rituals,
   e.g., Memorial Day, Thanksgiving Day

The AntiRitualist Case: Anarchism Reconsidered

Considering the anarchist attack on the state and on the "cult of authority," it is not strange that anarchists have focussed only on the repressive and reactionary aspects of ritual. The limitations of anarchism are nowhere more apparent, however, than in its diatribes against *all* forms of ritual. That negative theme is by now a familiar one. It begins with an overture attacking symbolic as opposed to direct action. Anarchists appear to assume that *all* ritual creates the illusion that one has done *something*, whereas, in fact, the world goes on as before; after the performance of the rite, the participants feel that they have done what they could to avert disaster and that nothing further can indeed be done. Of course, the anarchists lament the passivity of the masses who are all too ready to surrender control into the hands of one priesthood or another, for example, doctors with healing rituals, or teachers with rites of initiation into society. I am arguing, however, that some rituals do *not* habituate individuals to whatever devotion to authority society provides.

What appears arbitrary or open to revision becomes—through ritual—the right way of doing things; to ritualize conflict therefore trains the faithful only to ask for and to receive what various religious or secular priesthoods are prepared to offer. That is why the anarchist complaint against ritual issues a call for spontaneous action that will introduce genuine innovation to a society. Instead of the appearance of progress provided by ritual, in which individuals go through a prescribed sequence of motions in worship, learning, healing, or political action to a foreordained conclusion, anarchists would interrupt these proceedings in order to make room for genuine reconciliation and true innovation. Unless they are interrupted, rituals, secular or sacred, appear to create a world without outside connections, an imaginary world of pseudo-action that substitutes necessity for freedom. That world, however, *may* provide the seeds of revolutionary hope. Much depends on how sharply framed a ritual is, on its contrast with everyday life and the status quo.

In speaking of heroism, there is a tendency to elitism in anarchist thought, a belief that the future is in the hands of those who refuse to go the way of the horde. Anarchism can trace its roots to sectarian movements in the Middle Ages and early in the Reformation, to those who felt they could be saved from death and damnation without paying their liturgical or ecclesiastical dues. These roots are prophetic and profoundly antiritualistic. The same sectarianism underlies the anarchist revolt against the fathers of any society; witness the sectarian attack against the fathers in the university, the church, and the work place during the Reformation (Erikson 1958). In anarchist literature, there is occasionally an elitist tone that finds expression in a preference for creative genius or for minorities. To an American, schooled in the virtues of a liberal democracy, these words of Emma Goldmann pose a serious challenge:

> The living, vital truth of social and economic well-being will become a reality only through the zeal, courage, the non-compromising determination of intelligent minorities, and not through the mass.

> [The majority] has suppressed the human voice, subdued the human spirit, chained the human body. As a mass its aim has always been to make life uniform, gray, and monotonous as the desert (1969:78).

Patriotism, greed, unquestioning loyalty to the society and its central authority, and a chronic superstition that abandons one set of fears only to adopt another through a lifelong willingness to be spooked; these are the characteristics of a mass. No wonder that anarchists have been hostile to rituals that reinforce the masses' willingness to sacrifice themselves on the altar of the nation. Political rituals do express and yet disguise, resolve and yet never satisfy popular yearnings to be free; other rituals, however, may intensify the yearnings for liberation.

Goldmann's preference for the *active* minority helps to illustrate the anarchist hostility to rituals. Most rites fail to provide a clear outlet for an individual's particular will and purpose; instead, the participants come to see themselves as actors in a complex world that casts them in various roles without regard to their specific qualities or experiences. Rituals invoke a global set of causes that leave the individual per se little choice except to say Amen or to leave. Rites make it unnecessary for the *separate* individual to take a forthright and irreversible stand or to move uncompromisingly and alone toward a single goal, whatever the cost. Individuals who take part in rituals are even more likely to be duped by their social system than individuals who are part of the inert mass. I am arguing, however, that certain rituals, like death, may wonderfully concentrate the individual mind.

What Goldmann seeks is a person who does not sacrifice a grasp of reality—does not minimize the frightening aspects of the real world—but who nevertheless is capable of action without "faithless fears and worldly anxieties." Rites reinforce a collective but only magical conviction that frightening possibilities have causes and can be prevented or controlled. Spooked by their own fantasies of evil afoot in the world, the majority lag behind; that is why, as the proverb puts it, the devil takes the hindmost. Of course, there is a certain complexity in the mind and imagination of the individual, a complexity informed and intensified by culture. Once ritualized, a culture can further preoccupy and entrance the individual with imaginary threats and artificial rewards. Against this hyperdevelopment, Herbert Read makes the authentic anarchist objection.

> The whole of our capitalist culture is one immense veneer: a surface refinement hiding the cheapness and shoddiness at the heart of things.
> To hell with such a culture . . . the state of the world today is a sufficient comment on those traditional embodiments of wisdom, ecclesiastical or academic, which we are expected to honour (1963:30–31).

Here is the militant theme again. The anarchists' attack on ritual invokes the freedom of the individual to discover the world afresh, to find and to make things that are genuinely new, as well as to learn what is enduring and valuable about the practical culture of the past. Read (ibid.) has a preference for pots and pans, for thatching hay and crafting sonnets; beyond those fundamental crafts, the remainder of culture and technique is often an embroidering or embellishing of experience that makes for oppressive complexity. Rituals of the fourth type in my typology habituate the individual to such complexity and cause individuals to doubt their own perceptions; they may well blunt the impulse to make something, or to make something really happen (See table 1). Such rites encourage the individual to engage in the "auspicious reification" of experience (Johnson, 1977:147). Much depends on the degree of contrast between rituals and everyday social life.

Ritual may not only convince the individual of his or her own inadequacy, but may make it difficult for the individual to distinguish the self from the external world of objects and meanings (cf. Johnson 1977:149–51). Like the alienated individuals who keep reproducing the symptoms that they are attempting to express, interpret, or explain, the participants in a ritual may find it difficult to distinguish their own from others' convictions and experience. Rituals may dull a sense of what Stirner (1845, 1971:125) called "owness": a sense of the uniqueness of the self in terms that may never be understood and shared by others. The inner self then may become isolated and idiosyncratic in ritual, or merely fused with external people and things, a lonely and incommunicable self, or one that is wholly typical, or both. As Johnson puts it, to heighten a patient's awareness of how the inner world meshes with the outer world rather than to supply an empathy that assures the patient that he or she is both a separate person and yet well understood, can intensify an already chronic loneliness and isolation (1977:149). Ritual may create the passive and lonely mass of individuals who seek a cure for their alienation in ritualized social encounters.

The anarchist, in saying "to hell with culture," seeks to provide a world in which the basic necessities of life can be made, shared, used, and consumed without mystifying either what individuals have in common with one another or the past, and without making them more lonely and individualistic than they already are. As an all-embracing fiction that provides surrogate selfhood and imaginary communion, ritual must go. In its place, a society could do worse than make common things, like pots and pans, that are useful, beautiful, and enduring.

Read's comment about "capitalist culture" can be applied to

contrived, modern ceremonies of the types I have been considering, an "immense veneer: a surface refinement hiding the cheapness and shoddiness at the heart of things." In modern societies, rituals may reinforce the notion that things are not what they seem, that appearances are deceiving and people are phony. Indeed, writers like Riesman and Whyte have characterized this conviction in more sophisticated terms, such as "other-directed" and "organization man," and Mary Douglas (1970) has noted the widespread assumption that rituals are empty gestures. As Johnson (1977:141) points out, however, the experience of others as being "phony" or "plastic," and of social life itself as being inauthentic, characterizes alienated individuals, whether or not it also characterizes the "compact mass" or majority to which Goldmann referred so scathingly. Certainly, ritual *may* make individuals more aware of their alienation. Much depends on how tightly framed a ritual is, on whether the form and the content appear identical.

Johnson reminds us that individuals often become "distracted" by internal thoughts, images, and feelings, so much so that they cannot really entertain the thoughts and experiences of others, who increasingly seem as distracted, preoccupied, and self-conscious as the alienated individuals themselves. As a result, "Like "sincerity," spontaneity appears to be a meaningless word, since the schizoid person is so wretchedly aware of the mechanism underlying specific actions" (1977:141). It hardly seems possible that others could be "for real"; indeed, the individual finds it easier to act when he or she knows that it is only acting; less is at stake (Johnson 1977:140). The word often, and rightly, used to describe such a world is "ritualistic." In the most artificial and contrived ceremonies, individuals must indeed be aware of the proper sequence of actions, the right time to say the right words, and the appropriate gestures for each moment and occasion.

In the last analysis, however, anarchists are divided as to whether or not religion and ritual can provide an ally against the state or is merely a way to buttress the state's claims to authority. Certainly, the use of ritual by fascists and communists in Nazi Germany and Soviet Russia provides ample warning of the repressive aspects of ritual in the hands of state authority. What fascinated Kropotkin most about medieval cities was their capacity to resolve their own conflicts and to enter into new associations with one another without the benefit of external authorities; it was precisely in these two ways that ritual was of primary importance to the formation of liberated and interdependent cities in the West. As Kropotkin (1904) reminds us, when there was a quarrel among the cities or the guilds, the parties would go from one city to another to "seek the sentence," the words that would provide a formula for reconciliation on which all parties to the conflict could agree. In fact, that is precisely the core function of ritual—to provide a sentence that adjudicates a conflict either between parties or between parts of the self. The sought after sentence may therefore be one of absolution and remission, of blessing and pardon, of penalty and proper penance; in any event, it is historically the function of ritual to provide such an authoritative sentence that a conflict can be resolved. Indeed, according to Kropotkin, medieval cities formed their confraternities of trade and mutual assistance in a rite in which all parties to the new covenant agreed to suspend all prior quarrels and grievances; they buried the ceremonial hatchet, so to speak. The point is not only that ritual was of primary importance in initiating and maintaining free cities in the middle ages; it provided a framework that called for no outside intervention, and provided, therefore, no opportunity for the type of intervention that lead eventually to the centralization of military and political authority in Western societies, i.e., to the state itself.

Weber and the anarchists were right. The path from the medieval city to the modern bureaucratized society is a steep decline from relatively high levels of freedom and responsibility. What modern societies might have been was once visible in the more primitive forms of social organization that preceded the Reformation, the consolidation of principalities into nation states, and the spread of formal organizations. What modern societies might yet become is a question that cuts to the heart of the matter. How much indeed is it necessary to undo what has been done, to dismantle oppressive structures, to simplify what has become far too complex to be owned and controlled by any individuals acting either singly or together? If sociology cannot contribute to the discussion of these questions, it perhaps has ignored the contributions that a prophetic paradigm can make. Here, therefore, I have attempted to at least articulate an ideal, an end point from which to criticize a particular society and from which to analyze specific degrees of freedom and subordination, of domination and complexity. Utopias are out of sociological fashion, but I agree with Kropotkin that "mental timidity in constructing an ideal is certainly a criterion of mental timidity in practice" (1970:47).

Conclusion

Ritual initially belongs to the people and is only slowly appropriated by the king, who uses it to enhance, justify, and extend the powers of the state. Take, for example, Becker's argument about the social origins of inequality (1975:52–63). In the beginning, all that we can find are individuals trying to breathe life into the figures they create to reanimate the world. In reading Becker, we can almost imagine the original shaman taking a figure of clay, poking holes in it for eyes and a nose, and then breathing on it to give it life. Although Becker does not explicitly use the Genesis account of creation, that account does suggest that, at some moment not lost to our memory, individuals of extraordinary abilities were thought to be able to give images life; it is a short step to making images of animals and naming them. Primitives created the world in their own image, with their own breath, out of their own mouths, through their own speech. They spoke, as it were, and there was light and life. Of course such animism appeared to give them frightening powers that indeed frightened them. I would argue that their magic so awed them that they preferred to endow others with it rather than tremble at their own imaginary powers. First the shaman, perhaps; then a deity who, like the shaman, dwelled among them. One culture of which we have continuous records chose a god whose presence could not be assumed or demonstrated; Becker (1975:53) is quite clear that the Israelites were an anomaly among the primitives.

The procedures for transferring life from one person or figurine to another were early ritual, the magic of the people. Becker argues, as Kropotkin argued nearly one hundred years earlier, that the powerful learn to make their rule appealing and legitimate by donning the garbs of popular custom and by making the people's magic work for themselves. First, as guardians of custom, primitive chiefs became responsible for the fruits of magic—fertility, good crops, and protection against disaster. When the magic fails, the king must die. I have been arguing (a) that the rituals of the secular state have failed, (b) that the state must in some sense die if the nation is to live.

Becker goes on to recount, however, the increasing immunity of the chiefs—the transition from high responsibility to high office, from high office to the extension of that office, until the king's custom replaces the custom of the people. What the king prescribes becomes obligatory, the custom that must be performed, the right way of doing things, and the tribute that must be paid. People become mere customers of the king. It is time, I am suggesting, for tribute to be withheld from the state in order to restore control over ritual to the nation itself.

In speaking of the "evolution" of such inequality, Becker is really speaking of the way that the erotic, life-giving and life-enhancing drives of the people become repressed until those drives serve not only to bind the people together but to subordinate them to the few who manage the social system themselves. There are, no doubt, several stages by which such repression evolves. Becker (1975:52–53) mentions what well may be the first stage: the appearance of extraordinary individuals who appeared to have exceptional endowments of physical or spiritual power. No doubt, they received tribute and were ceded control over the performance of the people's magic. As these figures become indispensable to the effective performance of the community's rites in agriculture and warfare, they become entitled to a larger share of communal goods; at the same time, the tendency to pit rivals against each other in ritualized demonstrations of their power intensifies competition among the gifted and makes the winner's demands for a "lion's share" legitimate (ibid.:59). As power and wealth became concentrated in the hands of a few who performed important functions and won crucial tests, those figures were able to extend the range of their function and to successfully impose certain rites as a test of popular loyalty: "There was now nothing to stop the state from taking more and more functions and prerogatives into itself, from developing a class of special beings at the center and inferior ones around it, or from beginning to give these special beings a larger share of the good things of the earth" (Becker 1975:58). As a simple measure of the effects of this inequality, one might measure the length of skeletons of those individuals who, in recent excavations of primitive sites, were found nearest the king's grave or next to the cultic center of the community. No doubt those who lived—and were therefore buried—nearest to the center of things were better fed, lived longer, and achieved a physical stature commensurate with their social standing. As Becker (1975:58) reminds us, those farthest from the political and cultic center and lowest on the social ladder were not deemed even to have souls. When popular custom is taken over by the state, even the spirits of the people become expropriated. I have suggested that the emergence of heroic individuals may be necessary if conflict is to be ritualized in ways that do not serve the cult of political authority.

Now we can see precisely the logic in the argument of Kropotkin and others against the cult of authority. When individuals transfer the powers of life and death to a central institution, the state, and attribute to that institution powers that are as spiritual and magical as they are political and purely economic, the people literally become dispirited; they pay too much tribute to the state when the state takes their custom for its own purposes. A passive, disheartened people without a soul is a people that has had its spirit expropriated by the political center for the purpose of making the rulers' authority legitimate and expansive. No wonder that anarchism insists that people will only recover their own sense of power and authority when they refuse to pay economic and spiritual tribute to any political center.

Read states the anarchist credo thus:

> The whole case for anarchism rests on a general assumption . . . that the right kind of society is an organic being—not merely analogous to an organic being, but actually a living structure with appetites and digestions, instincts and passions, intelligence and reason. . . . Unless you can believe this, not as an ideal or fancy, but as a biological truth, you cannot be an anarchist (1954:50).

Unless we believe this, perhaps, we can never be truly free of the cult of authority. It is in any case one step—I would say the *next* step—to a secular society.

6 *Postscript*

To RITUALIZE SOCIAL CONFLICT may contribute, in the short run, to the formation of social authority and to its perpetuation in various forms of adoration or servitude, and I have been describing these forms as part of a "cult" of authority. In the long run, however, to ritualize social conflict inevitably fails. That is partly because *any* ritualized form of social life is like make-believe. It expresses and disguises certain motives and emotions that eventually will seek more direct and lasting satisfaction; many of these motives, moreover, are destructive, and the eventual breakdown of ritualized social encounters may cause the very pain and disturbance that ritual seeks to avoid. In this concluding postscript, I am arguing not only that rituals inevitably fail, but that there are aspects of modern societies that are particularly conducive to that failure. One such aspect is the context in which modern ritual must operate: a complex, shifting, and frustrating social context that makes any ritualized commitment or renunciation inevitably temporary and fragile. Another aspect of modern societies shows up in the rituals themselves. As I argued in the preceding chapter, the lack of a strong frame and a form tightly bound to specific contents makes modern ceremonials conspicuously make-believe—artificial and incomplete. There the point was made in connection with certain political rituals in the United States, Russia, and Nazi Germany. Here, I will turn for examples to recent revisions of the Book of Common Prayer in England and the United States. As discussion in this book began with the problem of sin, self-deception, remorse, and despair, it seems fitting to conclude with a few comments about the ritualized expression of guilt in these recently modernized ecclesiastical rites.

Before continuing with the discussion, it may help momentarily to review some of the ways in which modern societies, by ritualizing social conflict, not only perpetuate but intensify the motives of hatred and revenge. There is, indeed, something about modern societies that makes all of their ritualized expressions of conflict patently make-believe.

There is a reason to be wary of a society whose everyday or more formal rituals fail to provide a transforming metaphor for the stages of life and the succession of one generation and regime to another. Orderly, smooth, and efficient forms of social life disguise the difficulties a society may be having with progress. Ritualistic arrangements for taking on new roles, for instance, are difficult for some people all of the time, and for all people some of the time. Although regimes often will succeed other regimes, and one generation will succeed another smoothly, inevitably, and with more or less dignity, these orderly transitions, precisely because they are so orderly, may conceal hostility to all social authority. We are therefore too often surprised to find one regime finally succeeding another with bloodshed and with precious little dignity for those unfortunates who are banned or executed. We would be making a mistake to assume that succession from one stage in life to the next always will occur relatively on schedule; for some, the succession of life-stages is always too abrupt and difficult, and in the 1960s there was little that was effortless in the way an entire generation of young people came of age. When a generation ages too quickly, the transition is often violent, and even the normal course of activities seems meaningless or oppressive.

When educational curricula cease to offer a course to follow and become a set of options, the succession of work and play becomes problematical. Too many choices and too few requirements make any achievement suspect; one never knows when one has done enough or what one has accomplished. So long as individuals go quietly from work to play, job to job, and course to course, their underlying doubt and anger at facing a bewildering array of meaningless or hopeless choices need not trouble the public agenda. That hostility may never achieve public importance and may become merely a chronic, widespread disenchantment of the sort described by Lasch as "narcissim."

In extreme cases, the boundary between work and play disappears. For the experience of this extremity, Erik Erikson (1969) has given us a phrase, "identity crisis." Individuals who experience a breakdown in their ability to move from one stage in life to the next turn night into day; the normal succession of activities fails to engage them. At any given moment, they may not be sure what to do next, and they are notably unsure what to do with their lives. They seek an all-or-nothing fusion with roles, but fail to find a role to which they can make a total commitment. Individuals in "identity crisis" want everything to make sense; nothing else will do, and they would prefer nothing to a life that only makes partial sense. Under these conditions and for these people, ordinary roles fail to enable them to take their place in the succession of generations, and even rituals fail to inspire faith and give conviction. When some individuals find the ordering of activities and stages of life no longer attractive, routine decisions take on existential, life and death significance. At such times, individuals hunger for personal transformation. Individuals in such extremities may choose to enter any one of several highly ritualized social contexts, from the army to a religious sect.

To ritualize social conflict not only disguises, but aggravates the very real costs of leaving behind certain attachments and pursuing more distant or symbolic goals. It is costly for parents to train their children to lead lives in which the parents cannot directly share. It is costly to accept chronic, however mild, disenchantment with the appearances and rewards of social life, or to go through motions that no longer express genuine feelings and commitment. It is costly to live without common goals and aspirations. Abstract values and a consensus on the importance of progress can therefore create, at the very least, a marked ambivalence toward progress and its inevitable costs. In a social crisis, as it is with individuals undergoing crises in identity, a larger proportion of individuals may become unwilling to go through certain motions and to speak in prescribed ways without "meaning it" (Erikson 1962:70ff).

The promises of secular authorities will no longer ring true if a society faces irretrievable and perhaps catastrophic losses in accidents, through policies that require the use of lethal chemicals and nuclear energy, or war. The possibility of nuclear or chemical warfare underscores peacetime dangers and intensifies ambivalence toward progress. Even without such external threats, however, modern societies generate too much waste to make change appear to be "progress." In bad times or in times of mortal danger, ambivalence toward such costly progress will cease to be chronic and become acute.

Unresolved ties to people or places or to a way of life can prevent individuals from "getting on with it" and from acquiring new skills or satisfactions in life. In their study of working-class men from the Boston area, Sennett and Cobb (1966) repeatedly found individuals who despised their current work and surroundings despite the fact that these individuals had made very real progress in the form of additional education, income, or attainments in their jobs. Their lack of satisfaction became apparent as they reminisced about their parents' work. By comparison with their parents' labors, what they were now doing did not seem to be "real" work. Sometimes they looked on themselves as a sham or as not "having what it takes"; their origins, a family or community that they still held dear, were more real to them than their present social life in a college or middle-class suburb.

Finally, then, the small ceremonies that bind individuals together into a moral community of mutual respect, if not affection, may become so formal or fragile that they appear to be a sham or an imposition; they are thus easily ignored or broken. Individuals are thus left to their own devices to make up for their lost but still precious associations. Some yearning may take on the form of romantic seeking for lost loves. Some will turn to activities that promise a more concrete and direct connection with an object of desire; witness many a commercial that promises real connection and final release from the burdens of separate existence in an orgy of fun and convivial drinking. Under these conditions, it is difficult to see how a secularized society can bind people together into valued associations whose memories and hopes for progress transcend death.

The ritualization of social conflict allows grief and rage, hostility and greed to find only symbolic expression and partial satisfaction. Once ritualized, these emotions may be acted out in ways as harmless as entertainment and sport; in the more harmful but rationalized routines of the office or marketplace; or in even more direct forms of acting out in illness and violence. If the primitive survives in modern societies without the benefit and limits of adequate ritual, these destructive motives will cause untold damage and generate equally destructive reactions.

Of course, many people feel relatively trusting of one another, with no backlog of grievances to satisfy, and are relatively confident of their own futures; anger and hatred are likely to simmer quietly, if these emotions become conscious at all. But among people of opposing ethnic or racial groups, whose confidence is low and whose memories can recall ancient grievances, relative strangers can quickly learn to mistrust and even to hate one another. These latter emotions are likely to disrupt the fragile discourse of work or the marketplace, of politics in the state and even in the church.

Perhaps the most widespread disruption of social patterns in the United States during recent years was in the 1960s. Political dissidents interrupted courtroom ritual with disrespectful forms of address and by chanting "Om." Civil disobedience challenged the sacredness of the flag and of patriotic rites. The counterculture took liberties with grammar and syntax, linguistic institutions already under strain from administrative and technological neologisms. Rituals of greeting and forms of address were ignored or challenged in the classroom, on the street, and even within the family where patterns of domination by the older generation and by males faced challenges from women and the young. The problem is partly a reflection of the fact that the routines of everyday life in modern organizations cannot long contain the emotions that may destroy the social fabric beyond repair. The problem is perpetuated when these symbolic exchanges generate and perpetuate the very hatreds that they are meant to control.

The bureaucratic and political ritualization of social conflict is therefore self-defeating. Watergate becomes a national symbol, not simply because of official lies and theft, but because of official coverup and stonewalling. It takes time to see through the office or role, whether of President or bank manager, welfare administrator or police officer; officials' roles are like "covers" and stone walls. But when Nixon finally resigned from the Oval Office, the nation could see an individual who had hated his enemies, had wished to eliminate them, had observed few legal limits on the extension of his office's power, had felt the President to be above the law itself, and had acted as if he had fantasies of indestructibility or near omnipotence in the use of the armed forces for various "incursions." It is frightening for a nation to see itself "writ large" in a president who uses his office to express a hatred thinly disguised by language and lengthily defended by procedural arguments; it is especially frightening when one realizes that this man indeed "represents" the people themselves in their work and politics to the extent that their roles not only cover and preserve but exacerbate their own destructive motives and hostile intentions.

The bureaucratic ritualization of social conflict creates roles of unwitting victimizers, and categories of anonymous victims. One can act "as if" one is merely doing one's job or official duty when one is, in fact, acting out one's own hostile or aggressive wishes. By the making of policy, one can act impersonally to create or destroy; one can make new categories of persons eligible for service, or liable for punishment, or ineligible for official considerations. King David once was censured by the prophets for his presumptions in enumerating the people in his domain in an early taking of the census. Who will now judge the state for eliminating from its rolls thousands of individuals who, discouraged in the pursuit of jobs, drop from official enumerations of the "labor force" or, invisible in the inner city, drop from the census of citizens?

The count of citizens by the state raises up some people in various categories and eliminates, as though they were dead, thousands of others from the lists. What individuals may accomplish in their minds by magical thinking, *viz*, the disappearance of another person or even an entire group of persons, the state may now accomplish through the most routine actions.

The resulting demands for satisfaction and revenge are most apparent whenever recent insults have been added to memories of ancient injury. If there is again to be a widespread breakdown of social life in America during the 1980s, it will perhaps occur most acutely in the formal exchanges of blacks and whites. Women and youth, whose social experiences intensify their own grievances, may also provide an added dynamic alongside that of the black population. But blacks, with less to lose and more to gain than either the young or women, may well be the first to disrupt the symbolic exchanges of everyday life, if no longer at lunch counters and on buses, then once again in the offices or waiting rooms and on the streets. Such a breakthrough of suppressed hatred will place an enormous strain on the rituals that form the second line of defense against violence and vengeance and may call for new, collective forms of commitment, sacrifice, and national repentance.

In the previous chapter, I questioned whether political rites in modern nations are capable of providing the necessary transformations and social commitments. Certainly, in America, there is a dearth of adequate ritual at the national level; no wonder that some groups still wish that America could rid itself of certain impure elements in the body politic, perhaps through a final and violent confrontation. The self-esteem of certain groups is still threatened by the pride and grievances of native-Americans who resent being displaced from their ancestral lands onto reservations, or by those who have come only lately to American soil. The nation also had reason to fear the revenge of those it has wished to eliminate from its welfare obligations or as beneficiaries of its foreign policy. Vengeance only belongs to the Lord when, through ritual, the past can be completed and finished, done with and undone, transfigured once and for all. Where rituals fail, social life may for the time being preserve only a fragile civility.

More is missing in modern societies than an ennobling myth; what has disappeared is a ritual that will bind those who lead and those who follow in a single procession toward a common destiny. In this book, however, I have not joined in the sociological lament for rites that bind a national community in gestures of a common obedience to a transcendent authority. On the contrary, I have argued that objects of common devotion and leaders who inspire commitment are often profoundly "alienating." That is, followers invest such symbols and leaders with their own individual abilities, strengths, rights, and responsibilities. The leaders become invested with what the people fail to recognize in themselves— vision, authoritative and powerful speech, and the burden of finding the way forward. In more traditional societies and to some extent in modern ones as well, leaders become invested not only with a people's proper possessions but with their popular illusions, a sense of superior wisdom and strength and even a magical transcendence over death itself. Since individuals thus become alienated because they personify their own illusions and desires in external figures, all worship, whether of traditional deities or of celebrities and politicians, may become a source of alienation. The decline of ritualized forms of piety and obedience, whether in politics or academia, in the home or in the world of work, may therefore herald the day in which individuals and the populace rediscover themselves as the source of political authority. Although that outcome may be desirable, the way toward such a future is, I argue, perilous. It is perilous because individuals, groups, and even whole societies seek to precipitate tests of strength and to justify their claims in political trials or in trial by combat.

Pressures for trials of strength and virtue increase in the absence of successfully ritualized gestures and words that orient leaders and followers along a common path. Rituals enable leaders to point to new horizons while setting limits on exploration. The problem of the leader is to avoid leading followers astray or misleading them while nevertheless pointing the way into an unknown territory and an uncertain future. Leaders must innovate and yet keep control, explore new and complex paths without losing the way forward or the way through the labyrinth. New leaders are constantly emerging who ignore or challenge the established and ritualized patterns for following the leader, who point out new directions, innovate successfully, and seek to rise to new heights. Established leaders must compete with these rivals, maintain their capacity to set limits and control innovation, without losing their initiative. At the same time, however, they must prepare to introduce a new generation of leaders to positions at the front of the procession. Rituals often help to elicit commitments from the new generation of both leaders and followers, while preparing them both for whatever sacrifices may be required. To continue to lead, one must never arrive at the end, and yet keep the end in sight. To mobilize followers requires a language of shared vision, but to keep followers requires a language that permits a certain leeway, exhortations against digressions and error, and punishments for going too far astray. It is a language that can often be found in rituals. When it is lacking, we can expect conflict between generations of leaders, conflict that may take to the streets rather than to the courts.

The lack of adequate ritual at the level of the nation is particularly dangerous. Ernest Becker argues that humans generally need some "heroic belonging to a victorious cause" if they are to feel that their own lives are significant (1975, 1976:142). Their daily victories over despair require participation in a power and in a wholeness more glorious by far than their own achievements. Humans need to scapegoat if they lack an enemy. Survival itself adds savor to everyday life and a sense of triumph over one's enemies, but where rituals fail to offer transcendence, a nation will require repeated nourishment from fresh victories. The basic need to feel that one's life counts for something is, according to Becker, a reaction to the threat of cosmic insignificance and a breeding ground for continual struggles for supremacy.

The decline of British imperialism, the insult as well as the injury of Vietnam to American pride, however, and the new assertions of racial and national power from countries and peoples that have long been the objects of derision, commercial subjugation, or crusade have underminded Western confidence. No one needs here a new rehearsal of the statistics of decline and self-doubt. Becker reminds us that "a nation represents victory and immortality or it has no mandate to exist. It must give tangible, straightforward victories or its credit is dissipated in the hearts of all its citizens" (1975, 1976:117). No one who has endured such losses as those sustained by the English can feel that their nation's victories have been "tangible" or "straightfoward"; no more can Americans celebrate their own victories in Vietnam without regret or even remorse. Those who have read the war memorials that cover English walls, or who come across the military markers in English graveyards, can no longer be entirely sure about immortality when death's triumph is so minutely and extensively detailed. There is a limit to the efficacy of sacrifice in guaranteeing the soul of a nation, and Western nations may have reached that limit.

If Niebuhr is right, there are two sins which require collective expression: remorse over self-deception, and repentance for the sin of unbelief. If such collective expression is now called for, it may well be needed by the nation itself. The last few decades have been especially ruthless to national illusions, and nations have been extraordinarily ruthless in their demand for power and glory in the present, rather than in some distant future which is the object of faith alone. It is particularly strange, I suggest, that at such a time modern rites in the churches should be revised in ways that minimize rather than intensify the collective expression of guilt and remorse.

In the earlier versions of the Book of Common Prayer, for instance, the words of the "general confession" were poignant and, by modern tastes, extreme in their expression of remorse and sinfulness.

> We have erred and strayed from the ways like lost sheep.
> We have followed too much the devices and desires of our own hearts.
> We have done that which we ought not to have done, and
> we have left undone that which we ought to have done.
> And there is no health in us.
> But thou, O Lord, have mercy upon us, miserable offenders.

These are not words that come easily to people who believe that they are basically healthy and can improve their individual and collective lives by various pragmatic strategies. Instead of these anguished statements of a people who have committed lèse-majesté against the divine sovereignty and parricide against a heavenly parent, the modern rites simply acknowledge failure in "thought, word, and deed"; a fairly matter of fact and terse statement.

No doubt, when compared with genuine honesty among people who have no illusions and are not subservient, rituals are an impediment both to progress, and to honest, trusting relationships. Indeed, I have been arguing that to ritualize social conflict gives the illusion of honesty and reconciliation rather than the substance of personal integrity or social change. It is a barrier to progress when individuals cover their real motives with pious, if self-accusatory, liturgical phrases. Instead of providing realistic expression of sinfulness and a more hopeful orientation toward the future, any rite, modern or not, may allow individuals to make melodramatic but self-deluding expressions of self-accusation and of hope for progress. Instead of giving Christians a chance to experience their true selves, the Church provides them with the experience of confessing a little bit of guilt. In return, the Church provides a little hope, not enough to provide a new birth, but simply a measure of temporary relief.

In a most telling piece on "psychological objections" to Christian, or rather to ecclesiastical, piety, H.A. Williams (1964:35–36) once argued that the churches substitute pious guilt for real guilt, trivial knowledge of one's sin for a thoroughgoing knowledge of one's inner self; he was speaking, furthermore, of the older Book of Common Prayer. The inner self, Williams, argued, will not so easily be fooled or disguised; at some level individuals know that they are not making a full confession when they accept the simple ABCs of Christian confession and pious resolution. Others also know that the devout are finding outlets for aggression in their acts of charity; this pious charade

> is the result of my never going deep enough into myself to discover the real cause of my aggressiveness. So the engine of aggressiveness races on as before. But what it produces is no longer open and above board. Instead it produces an extremely strained meekness and mildness. . . . Yet Christians are often so pathologically intent on preserving as far as they can an image of themselves as Christ-like, that they are totally unaware of the harm their attempted humility is doing to other people (ibid.:46–47).

The aggressive motive arising from cannabilistic or incestuous wishes escapes the notice of the self who lives according to the rules of Christian piety.

The alternative is a real transfiguration, what Williams calls a "genuine death to a false image" of oneself and "a genuine birth" to what one genuinely is (ibid.:48). Williams found particular fault with the confessions in the old Book of Common Prayer, but his quarrel is with ritual itself. Ritual evokes or provides a small enough dose of anxiety or guilt to be tolerable: The fear of damnation or the suggesion of inner corruption is enough to provoke

> what William Blake called the Nobodaddy—Nobody's daddy, He who is not. Even mild, gentlemanly, sober, cautious, exhortations about sin give Nobodaddy his opportunity. In Blake's words—"The Nobodaddy aloft farted and belched and coughed." And the result is we feel it absolutely necessary to placate him. And here is the deadly opportunity for effective evangelism. We have been brought under old Nobodaddy's spell, and towards him we insinuate, flatter, blow and bend the knee. (If you want to know what I mean read Cramner's two general confessions in the Book of Common Prayer.) But hope is offered to us. We shall be saved if we do what we are told (ibid.:51).

If this is true of the older, more intense expression of guilt in the Book of Common Prayer, it is far more true in the recent, truncated confessions.

While I would argue that any rite, and not only the modern ones, is only a poor substitute for genuine *personal* conversion and wholehearted contrition, ecclesiastical rites are not a substitute for the *individual's* confession and self-awareness, but merely a "general confession" of their common faults; not their inward guilt alone, but the *collective* failure of the people of God.

In any event, collective expressions of remorse have fallen out of fashion. The United States, which used to have a national day of repentence and thanksgiving, has engaged for the last century only in a day of thanksgiving without repentance. The church would appear to have cut its emotional ties with the nation enough, however, so that it could supply the mood of repentance that is missing in the political rites of the nation. Certainly, the American Episcopal church, at least, saw its life as separate from the nation; indeed, the Standing Liturgical Commission announced that, "After sixteen centuries since the time of Constantine, the Church is once again placed on a level with the dispossessed and the powerless." (Statement to the House of Bishops, October 1972, by Chilton Powell, Massey Shepherd, Charles Guilbert, and Leo Melania, p. 6). That statement did not mean that the Church had sold its real estate and given away its investment portfolios, but simply that it no longer felt it could enjoy the protections of a society that valued its contributions while giving only lip service to its values. Given what the Church thought was its mission to lead its people out of their various captivities, the Church might well have wanted a more searing confession of collective and *national* failure. In this century, there are particularly good reasons for a strong statement of collective sadness, and even remorse. Why, then, did the Church propose to adopt a more sanguine mood?

There are enough voices on this subject to make my own comment unnecessary, and one of those voices in particular supplies this *crie de coeur:*

> If we must change, why not change to the words of Scripture rather than substitute our own perfunctory admission that we have not done good? The point of the confessions is that we cannot do so without God's help. And in the age of the concentration camps, of the H-bomb, Vietnam, Ulster, universal terrorism, universal disorder, why should we resent a confession of our own part in all these as miserable offenders against the truth of perfection which is what our faith asserts? (Trickett 1981:71).

It is a cry for *collective* repentence that could have moved the Church to voice its sorrows in order that one day it may sound a note of common rejoicing. Without a strong expression of collective guilt, the voice of collective thanksgiving inevitably sounds brassy and self-congratulatory.

Since it considered itself at one with the dispossessed, the Episcopal Church could have led the nation in collective remorse and atonement, for instance, for the lives of Indochinese and Americans squandered in the Vietnam war. Instead, the Standing Liturgical Commission decided that the Church is now living in a different "culture" than the one in which the Book of Common Prayer was first written (1662) and cited a number of sociological factors to make their point. For instance, the Commission thought liturgical references to "foe" or "peril" were out of place in a world where dangers are more general or abstract and city streets are lighted at night by electricity (Memorandum 9, June, 1970:3, 35–36). Unfortunately, there is nothing general or abstract about napalm and dioxin; only the terms of American foreign policy speak of abstract dangers like the domino effect, world communism, and credibility.

It might seem that a secularized rite is all that is necessary in a modern society so fragmented and open to continuing exchange. Certainly partial and temporary actions seem to be all that is currently possible in the liturgy as well as in politics. But even modern societies require real transformation if they are to resolve hatred and grievances without action that is both direct and violent. A society that cannot transform cannot promise more in the way of a victory over death than a minor accommodation and a realistic outlook. In the normal course of events, and in relatively good times, such an outlook may be sufficient. On more challenging occasions, a society may need a more transfiguring vision. As custodians of such a vision, rituals provide needed reserves of faith and hope, but secularized rites provide no such vision, no untapped reservoir of courage. On the contrary, such rights dim that vision and erode those reserves.

Certainly the makeshift ceremonies of a secular society are hardly adequate to still the passions of conflict and of war itself. Lifton (1973:123ff.) has noted that American society lacks the rituals necessary to purify those who, like veterans returning from Vietnam, have been contaminated by their contact with death and who remind Americans of their collective responsibility for a vast tragedy. The routines of work and everyday life will not keep people at a safe distance from each other. Indeed, contact has already brought rage and recrimination from these veterans into the political arena, where it may find more potent expression and demand more costly sacrifices to justify lives already wasted and perhaps beyond redemption. Murderous rage or simple pleasure in killing, once acted out, present a danger of pollution at least as deadly as Agent Orange.

Opportunities for collective aggression have outstripped modern societies' capabilities for "collective catharsis" (Fanon, 1967:145). Granted that demonstrations in the 1960s provided momentary forms of cathartic action in the streets of America. Granted that riots vented passions that might otherwise have destroyed more lives and fewer buildings. Still, American society itself lacks the "second line of defense" that many a community has long since possessed in the way of effective collective ritual. The anger and the grievances that build up over many generations and are still remembered in many quarters cannot be satisfied by ordinary social or political action; neither can the mass media help, no matter how many black villains are slain in sagas of outer space. A society that fails to call its authorities adequately to account for their acts generates a destructive religious impulse.

Of course, we can see this impulse in the proclamations of apocalyptic sects that the world is facing Armageddon. A more subtle rendering of this demand comes from the conservative religious groups in the United States that anticipate a new era to emerge from Israel's forthcoming confrontations with her enemies—a confrontation foretold in the Biblical record as ushering in a millenium in which God's people shall sit in judgment over the peoples of the world. Some religious communities operate with a somewhat different notion of how God has judged the world, a more or less "realized" eschatology in which the divine judgment has already been given in the crucifixion and resurrection. These groups and organizations are therefore more likely to spell that judgment out in warnings and reprimands to the state than to await a forthcoming trial of faith. The Catholic Bishops, for instance, have recently issued their separate statements on the morality of using nuclear weapons at first or at all. These religious impulses, although they assume different timetables for divine judgment, acknowledge a strong and probably increasing public demand for judgment on the acts of sovereign authorities.

To some it may seem unnecessary to fear a resurgence of militant religion and messianic impulses in modern societies. Indeed, the detachment of individuals from their roles in everyday life requires no theater for special ordination, no extraordinary commissioning to such roles within a liturgical context. A simple renewal of one's decision to do one's best will suffice—most of the time—in most organizations. Modern rituals in fact succeed in doing little, since little in the way of the heroic is required of them. The battle with the enemies of faith is postponed to the end-time; the mean-time is a time indeed for moderation in all things.

Modern rituals no longer control the myths that promise a heroic consummation of the struggle of the saints. The myths of Armageddon and of cosmic heroism, once contained within the framework of ritual, now find a nonliturgical outlet through many channels, including the mass media. Television evangelists may stir their audiences to demand a final rapture, a once and for all showdown with the enemies of the new Israel. Modern audiences can talk themselves into Armageddon when the emotions raised by battle myths have no regular liturgical expression. Their dreams may indeed come true.

Bibliography

Bateson, Gregory, D. D. Jackson, J. Haley, and J. H. Weakland. "A Note on the Double-Bind-1962," in *Communication, Family, and Marriage*. Palo Alto, Calif.: Science and Behavior Books, 1970.

Becker, Ernest. *Escape from Evil*. New York: The Free Press, 1975.

Bellah, Robert N. "The Civil Religion," *Daedalus* (Winter 1967).

Berger, Peter L. *Invitation to Sociology: A Humanistic Perspective*. Garden City, N.Y.: Doubleday and Co., Anchor Books, 1963.

Bernstein, Basil. *Class, Codes and Control*, Vol. 3. *Towards a Theory of Educational Transmissions*. London, Boston, and Henley: Routledge and Kegan Paul, 1975.

Bourdieu, Pierre. *Outline of a Theory of Practice*. Cambridge, Mass.: Cambridge University Press, 1977.

———. and Jean-Claude Passeron. *Reproduction in Education, Society, and Culture*. Beverly Hills, Calif.: Sage Publishers, 1977.

Bakunin, Mikhail A. *Bakunin on Anarchy* (edited, translated, and with an Introduction by Sam Dolgoff). New York: Alfred A. Knopf, 1972.

Coles, Robert and Jane Hallowell Coles. *Women of Crisis: Lives of Struggle and Hope*. New York: Dell Publishing Company, 1978.

Collins, Randall. *Conflict Sociology: Toward an Explanatory Science*. New York, San Francisco, and London: Academic Press, 1975.

D'Aquili, Eugene G., Charles D. McLaughlin, John McManus, with Tom Burns, et al. *The Spectrum of Ritual*. New York: Columbia University Press, 1979.

Dobbelaere, Karel. "Secularization: A Multi-Dimensional Concept," *Current Sociology* 29 (2) (Summer 1981). Beverly Hills, Calif.: Sage Publishers.

Dolgoff, Sam (ed.). *Bakunin on Anarchy: Selected Work by the Activist-Founder of World Anarchism*. New York: Alfred A. Knopf, 1972.

Douglas, Mary. *Natural Symbols: Explorations in Cosmology*. New York: Random House, Vintage, (1970), 1973.

Durkheim, Emile. *The Division of Labor in Society Adulthood: Essays by Erik H. Erikson, et al*. New York: Norton, 1978.

———. "Identity and the Life-Cycle." Monograph, *Psychological Issues* I (1). New York: International Universities Press, 1969.

———. *Young Man Luther: A Study in Psychoanalysis and History*. New York: Norton, 1962.

Etzioni, Amitai, "Basic Human Needs, Alienation and Inauthenticity," *American Sociological Review* 33 (6):870–84.

173

Fanon, Frantz. *Black Skins, White Masks*. New York: Grove Press, 1967.
———. *The Wretched of the Earth*. New York: Grove Press, (1963), 1965.
Ferenczi, Sandor. *Further Contributions to the Theory and Technique of Psychonalysis*. New York: Boni and Liveright, 1927.
Freud, Sigmund. *Character and Culture*. New York: Collier Books, 1963.
———. *Civilization and Its Discontents*. New York: W. W. Norton and Co., 1962.
Fromm, Eric. *The Forgotten Language: An Invitation to the Understanding of Dreams, Fairy Tales, and Myths*. New York: Rinehart and Winston, 1957.
———. *Escape from Freedom*. New York: Farrar and Rinehart, Inc., 1941.
Giddens, Anthony. *Sociology: A Brief but Critical Introduction*. New York: Harcourt, Brace Jovanovich, Inc., 1982.
Glasner, Peter E. *The Sociology of Secularization: A Critique of a Concept*. Boston, Mass.: Routledge and Kegan Paul, 1977.
Goffman, Erving. *Forms of Talk*. Philadelphia, Pa.: University of Pennsylvania Press, 1981.
Goldmann, Emma. *Anarchism and Other Essays*. New York: Dover Publications, Inc., 1969.
Goodman, Paul. *New Reformation: Notes of a Neolithic Conservative*. New York: Random House, 1970.
———. *People or Personnel*. New York: Random House, 1963.
Greeley, Andrew. *Religion: A Secular Theory*. New York: The Free Press, 1982.
Hammond, Philip E. (ed.). *The Sacred in a Secular Age: Toward Revision in the Scientific Study of Religion*. Berkeley, Calif.: University of California Press, 1985.
———. and William Cole. "Religious Pluralism, Legal Development, and Societal Complexity," *Journal for the Scientific Study of Religion* 13:177–89 (1974).
Herberg, Will. *Protestant, Catholic, Jew: An Essay in American Religious Sociology*. Garden City, N.Y.: Doubleday, 1955.
Huntington, Richard and Peter Metcalf. *Celebrations of Death: The Anthropology of Mortuary Ritual*. Cambridge, Mass.: Cambridge University Press, 1979.
Illich, Ivan. *Deschooling Society*. New York: Harper and Row Publishers, Colophon Books, (1970), 1983.
Johnson, Benton, "A Fresh Look at the Concept of Secularization." Paper presented at the Annual Meeting of the Society for the Scientific Study of Religion, 1979.
Johnson, Frank A. "The Existential Psychotherapy of Alienated Persons," in Nelson, Benjamin (ed.), *The Narcissistic Condition*. New York: Human Sciences Press, 1977.
Keniston, Kenneth. *Young Radicals: Notes on Committed Youth*. New York: Harcourt Brace and World, 1968.
Klein, Melanie. *Contributions to Psychoanalysis 1921–1945*. London: Hogarth Press and Institute of Psychoanalysis, 1950.

Kozol, Jonathan. *The Night is Dark and I am Far From Home: A Political Indictment of the U.S. Public Schools.* New York: Continuum, (1975), 1980.

Kropotkin, Peter. *Revolutionary Pamphlets* (edited by Roger N. Baldwin). New York: Dover Publications, (1927), 1970.

———. *Selected Writings on Anarchism and Revolution* (edited by Martin A. Miller). Cambridge, Mass. and London, England: M.I.T. Press, 1970.

———. *Memoirs of a Revolutionist* (edited by James Allen Rogers). Garden City, N.Y.: Doubleday and Co., Inc., 1962.

———. *Mutual Aid.* London: Heinemann, 1904.

Lane, Christel. *The Rites of Rulers: Ritual in Industrial Society: The Soviet Case.* Cambridge, England, and New York: Cambridge University Press, 1981.

Lasch, Christopher. *The Culture of Narcissism.* 1969. New York: Norton, 1978.

Lifton, Robert J. *The Life of the Self: Toward a New Psychology.* New York: Basic Books, Inc., (1976), 1983.

———. *Home From the War.* New York: Simon and Schuster, 1973.

———. *Boundaries: Psychological Man in Revolution.* New York: Simon & Schuster, 1967.

Luhmann, Niklas. *The Differentiation of Society.* (Translated by Stephen Holmes and Charles Larmore.) Columbia University Press, 1982.

Marcuse, Herbert. *One Dimensional Man: Studies in the Ideology of Advanced Industrial Society.* Boston, Mass.: Beacon Press, (1964), 1968.

Martin, David A. *The Dilemma of Contemporary Religion.* New York: St. Martin's Press, 1981.

———. *A General Theory of Secularization.* New York: Harper and Row, 1978.

———. "Christianity and the Nation," mimeographed essay, London, 1981.

——— ed. *No Alternative:* The Prayer Book Controversy. With Peter Mullen, Oxford: Blackwell, 1981.

Nelson, Marie Coleman (ed.). *The Narcissistic Condition. A Fact of Our Lives and Times.* New York: Human Sciences Press, 1977.

Niebuhr, Reinhold. *The Nature and Destiny of Man: A Christian Interpretation,* Vols. I and II. New York: Charles Scribner's and Sons, 1953.

———. *The Irony of American History.* New York: Charles Scribner's and Sons, 1952.

———. *Faith and History.* New York: Charles Scribner's and Sons, 1951.

———. *An Interpretation of Christian Ethics.* New York and London: Harper and Brothers, Publishers, 1935.

O'Keefe, Daniel Lawrence. *Stolen Lightning.* New York: Random House, Vintage Books, 1983.

Read, Herbert. *The Cult of Sincerity.* New York: Horizon Press, 1969.

———. *Selected Writings of Herbert Read.* New York: Horizon Press, 1964.

———. *To Hell With Culture.* New York: Schocken Books, 1963.

———. *Anarchy and Order.* London: Faber and Faber, Limited, 1954.

———. *A Coat of Many Colours.* London: Routledge and Sons, 1945.

Riesman, David. *The Lonely Crowd: A Study of the Changing American Character* (with Rewel Denning and Nathan Glazer). New Haven, Conn.: Yale University Press, 1950.

Robertson, Roland. *The Sociological Interpretation of Religion.* New York: Schocken Books, 1970.

Rubenstein, Richard. *The Cunning of History.* New York: Harper and Row, 1975.

Schell, Jonathan. *The Fate of the Earth.* New York: Avon, 1982.

Sennett, Richard and Jonathan Cobb. *The Hidden Injuries of Class.* New York: Alfred A. Knopf, (1966), 1972.

Shils, Edward. *Center and Periphery: Essays in Macrosociology.* Chicago and London: University of Chicago Press, 1975.

Silverman, Lloyd H., Frank M. Lachmann, and Robert H. Milich. *The Search for Oneness.* New York: International Universities Press, Inc., 1982.

Stirner, Max. *The Ego and His Own* (edited by John Carroll). New York: Harper and Row, 1971.

Trickett, Rachel. "Cranmer Not Irrelevant," in Martin, David and Peter Mullen (eds.), *No Alternative.* Oxford: Basil Blackwell, 1981.

Turner, Victor. *The Ritual Process.* Hawthorne, N.Y.: Aldine, 1969.

Van Gennep. *Rites of Passage* (translated by M. B. Vizedom and G. Caffee with an Introduction by S. T. Kimball). Chicago, Ill.: University of Chicago Press, 1960.

Whyte, William H. *The Organization Man.* New York: Simon and Schuster, 1956.

Williams, H. A. "Psychological Objections," in MacKinnon, D. M., H. A. Williams, A. R. Vidler, and J. S. Bezzant, *Objections to Christian Belief.* Philadelphia, Pa. and New York: J. B. Lippincott Co., 1964.

Williams, Robin M. *American Society: A Sociological Interpretation* (3rd ed.). New York: Alfred A. Knopf, 1970.

Wilson, Bryan. "Secularization," in Hammond, Philip E. (ed.). *The Sacred in a Secular Age: Toward Revision in the Scientific Study of Religion.* Berkeley, Calif.: University of California Press, 1985.

———. *Religion in Sociological Perspective.* Oxford, England, and New York: Oxford University Press, 1982.

———. *The Magic and the Millennium.* London: Heinemann Education Books, 1973.

Wilson, John F. *Public Religion in American Culture.* Philadelphia, Pa: Temple University Press, 1979.

Winnicott, D. W. *The Child, The Family, and The Outside World.* England and New York: Harmondsworth, 1974.

Woodcock, George. *Anarchism: A History of Libertarian Ideas and Movements.* Cleveland, Ohio and New York: Meridian Books, 1962.

Zweig, Paul. *The Heresy of Self-Love.* Princeton, N.J.: Princeton University Press, (1968), 1980.

Index